Stylish
SUCCULENT
DESIGNS
& Other Botanical Crafts

Stylish
SUCCULENT
DESIGNS
& Other Botanical Crafts

40 DIF
Arrangements, Wreaths, Living Walls & More!

Jessica Cain, *founder of* In Succulent Love

PAGE STREET
PUBLISHING CO.

PAGE STREET
PUBLISHING CO.

First published in 2019 by
Page Street Publishing Co.
27 Congress Street, Suite 105
Salem, MA 01970
www.pagestreetpublishing.com

Distributed by Macmillan, sales in Canada by The Canadian Manda Group.

23   22   21   20   19   1   2   3   4   5

ISBN-13: 978-1-62414-845-3
ISBN-10: 1-62414-845-X

Library of Congress Control Number: 2019932995

Cover and book design by Kylie Alexander for Page Street Publishing Co.
Photography by Rachael Smith

Printed and bound in China

To My Grandma

Thank you for playing with me in the garden when I was growing up and inspiring my creativity. Thank you for teaching me how to make succulent pumpkins, which blossomed this whole journey I am now on. I will always cherish our crafting times together and look forward to what we create next. Thank you for being my friend, my supporter, my inspiration and my grandmother. I love you always.

Table of Contents

Introduction

Hello hello,

Thank you for choosing my book to begin, accelerate or complement your crafting! I am so excited to see what you create and what other inspirations come about! In this book, I have chosen 40 of my favorite botanical projects for you to make. They feature mostly succulent crafts, with the addition of some air plants and other botanicals. I encourage you to use full creativity in your arrangements, making them your own! All projects can be arranged with a variety of plants, various color themes and different vessels. I like to think of this as a "succulent cookbook," presenting you with all the techniques to craft your own botanical treasures. Of course, there are "recipes" to follow, but as with a cookbook, you can make each project unique!

Throughout the book, I use botanical names for the plants, but I also include their common names when available. For example, *Othonna capensis* is better known as 'Ruby Necklace', so keep this in mind when searching for succulent varieties. The botanical name will always be in italics, with the common name in single quotations.

I started my business, In Succulent Love, completely by accident, just by making succulent pumpkins (page 75) each fall with my grandmother. My succulent pumpkins quickly became popular, and orders started coming in. One thing led to another, and here I am . . . living this succulent-obsessed life, designing elaborate arrangements, covering walls with colorful plants, teaching people how to craft through DIY parties, shipping thousands of succulents throughout the country and now writing this book.

I hope that you fall in love with succulents, just as I did, and learn to create your own designs!

Much love and happy crafting,

Jessica Cain

www.insucculentlove.com
Instagram: @insucculentlove

There are many different types of succulent families, but these are five that stand out from the rest and make the perfect arranging succulents.

Aeonium: *Aeonium* succulents often have thinner leaves and rosette faces and thrive best during the winter months. They tend to propagate best when the heads are cut and planted, rather than by leaf propagation. *Aeonium* succulents thrive in full sun, partial sun and some shaded locations. Most grow upward rather than spreading out. They are a favorite of mine in designs due to their flowerlike nature. They can be used as a great alternative to fresh flowers! This arrangement is composed of *Aeonium* 'Kiwi', *Aeonium* 'Fiesta' and *Aeonium* 'Mardi Gras' (in the center).

Crassula: *Crassula* succulents are some of the hardiest succulents out there. They make the perfect fillers in arrangements. A common one is the jade plant, which comes in a vast variety of colors and variations. *Crassula* succulents can be neglected due to their forgiving nature. They can be reproduced by leaf propagation, as well as cuttings. This arrangement is composed of *Crassula* 'Tom Thumb', *Crassula* 'String of Buttons', *Crassula perforata variegata* and *Crassula argentea variegata* 'White Jade'.

Echeveria: *Echeveria* succulents are my personal favorite. They come in almost every color, and they grow big and beautiful! They are the perfect eye-catching part of any succulent design. Most can be beheaded, meaning that if you cut the top off, over time, the plant will produce babies on the stem you originally cut from. Leaf propagation and cuttings are additional ways to reproduce these succulents. This arrangement is composed of *Echeveria* 'Perle Von Nürnberg' ('PVN'), *Echeveria* 'Neon Breaker', *Echeveria* 'Lilacina' and *Echeveria* 'Sanyatwe'.

Sedum: *Sedum* succulents are also perfect fillers for all types of arrangements. They are available in ground cover flats, which can be split up to make arrangements. *Sedum* succulents reproduce often and are also very easy to grow. Most thrive in full sun and bright-light locations. They can be propagated by cuttings and by leaf propagation. This arrangement is composed of *Sedum reflexum* (in the back), followed by *Sedum* 'Pink Jelly Beans' and *Sedum* 'Donkey Tail' (cascading over the front).

Senecio: *Senecio* are often trailing succulents, making them a go-to in arranging. They are also commonly found in varying hues of green and blue, some of which come in ground covers. Drainage is particularly important for these succulents, as they can rot very easily. They thrive on staying dry. This arrangement is composed of *Senecio* 'String of Pearls' cascading over the edges of the Mason jar.

Supplies, Techniques
AND ARRANGING METHODS

Soil: I recommend using cactus soil for all of the planting projects in this book. Various garden stores or home improvement stores sell cactus soil in their soil sections (some may label it as succulent soil). To make your own, simply mix equal parts regular soil and pumice or perlite. It is important for the succulents to have lots of drainage in the soil, which is why cactus soil is used.

Pumice: Pumice is crumbled volcanic rock that will absorb excess water and slowly filtrate it back into soil over time. Using pumice as a top dressing or mixed into soil is a healthy complement for succulents. Utilizing pumice at the bottom of planters and pots without drainage holes is an excellent alternative to drilling holes. I like working with the ⅛" (3 mm) and ³⁄₁₆" (5 mm) pieces of pumice from General Pumice Products.

Chopsticks: Chopsticks are a great tool for arranging smaller plants or for planting tight designs. When adding succulents to soil, use chopsticks to finely nudge the succulents close to others.

Misting Bottle: Misting bottles are always on my worktable, filled with water, as they are often utilized for spraying the tops of arrangements. When I finish arrangements, I gently mist them with water to brush away excess soil in the middle of the plants. I also use misting bottles to spray the soil before planting, if it is overly dry. Working with moist soil is easier in arranging. Misting bottles are also a great tool to water succulents and air plants.

Water Squeeze Bottle: Garden squeeze bottles are useful for larger arrangements. Gently squeeze the water onto the larger plants to remove soil from them. Or use the bottles' fine tips to water plants.

Tongs: Tongs are long tweezers commonly used in arranging. They are a go-to for all small arrangements. Using tongs can help fit small plants into tighter locations that our fingers may be too big for. I also use tongs to add top-dressing accessories in small areas.

Mini Garden Shovel: In small arrangements, using a mini shovel is another easy way to get into locations tight for planting. I always have various sizes of shovels near my workspace, but my favorites are 1- and 2-inch (2.5- and 5-cm)-wide mini shovels to get into tight spaces!

Rust-Oleum®: For all metal containers, I recommend using Rust-Oleum clear spray paint prior to planting. This will help ensure that the metal planters will not rust over time.

Hot Glue: Hot gluing succulents onto moss will not prevent the succulents from growing. The glue is used to adhere the succulents in place; then they will start to root directly into the moss. When gluing succulents, it is crucial that they are secure, so sometimes using an extra layer of glue is helpful. To hot glue succulents, simply add hot glue in the location of your desire, then place the succulent stem in the hot glue, add additional hot glue on top of the stem and quickly cover it with moss. Press the moss onto the stem with the hot glue, holding it until it is dry. Before finishing the craft, gently wiggle each succulent to make sure it is secure. If the succulents are still slightly loose, add an extra layer of glue and moss.

Tacky Glue: Tacky glue can be used in lieu of hot glue, following the same method. Using tacky glue is more time consuming because it does not dry as fast, but it will work the same as hot glue.

Floral Wire: Another method of attaching succulents to various arrangements is to hand wire the succulents onto the vessel. This method works if the succulents will be living in moss. To wire a succulent in moss, take the stem of a succulent, add moss on top of the stem and then wrap floral wire around the moss several times. Add more moss on top of the wire, then wrap the wire an additional time around the stem to secure the succulent.

Planting: Planting succulents can be done by planting the entire plant with the roots attached or by planting cuttings. To plant cuttings, simply snip off a cutting from another succulent, then place the stem in soil. Depending on the type of succulent, roots will form within 1 to 3 weeks. Succulents are not overly fast-growing plants, so planting them in close proximity to one another is okay.

Arranging: In typical floral arranging and plantscaping, it is best to use a thriller, a filler and a spiller plant. The thriller plant is the most vibrant and eye-catching plant out of the arrangement. The filler plant is usually a larger plant that is leafier, taking up more room in the arrangement. The spiller plant is usually the plant that will spill and cascade over the side of the arrangement. In the arrangement to the left, the *Senecio* 'String of Pearls' is the "spiller," the *Portulacaria afra variegata* 'Rainbow Bush' is the "filler" and the *Kalanchoe luciae variegata* 'Fantastic' is the "thriller."

Since an odd number of plants is always best in arranging, I suggest using all three—a thriller, a filler and a spiller—in the arrangement. Using multiples of the thrillers, fillers and spillers can make for a unique design—just make sure you use an odd number of plants. When selecting plants, it is crucial to pair together plants that have similar needs for light and moisture.

- **Thriller Succulent Recommendations:** *Aeonium* 'Sunburst', *Echeveria* 'Sahara', *Echeveria* 'Afterglow', *Echeveria* 'Perle Von Nürnberg' ('PVN'), *Echeveria* 'Cassyz Winter', *Echeveria* 'Cubic Frost' or any bright or bold succulent that stands out against the others.

- **Filler Succulent Recommendations:** *Sedum* 'Pink Jelly Beans', *Sedum reflexum*, *Sedum confusum*, *Crassula argentea variegata* 'White Jade', *Oscularia deltoides* or any plant that has several stems or multiheads.

- **Spiller Succulent Recommendations:** *Xerosicyos danguyi* 'String of Coins', *Senecio* 'String of Pearls', *Sedum* 'Donkey Tail', *Senecio* 'String of Bananas', *Othonna capensis* 'Ruby Necklace', *Peperomia* 'Ruby Cascade', *Cotyledon pendens* 'Cliff Cotyledon', *Senecio jacobsenii* 'Trailing Jade' or any succulents that cascade and trail downward.

1 gallon (4 L)

6 inch (15 cm)

4 inch (10 cm)

2 inch (5 cm)

$\mathscr{S}$tatement PIECES

A statement piece is a work of art that is breathtaking—a one-of-a-kind conversation starter. In this chapter, I showcase my favorite project to date: a Succulent Fountain (page 31) full of cascading succulents and bright pops of pink! I'll also teach you to transform an old birdbath into a classy Succulent Birdbath (page 33). Learn how to craft your own Succulent Driftwood Tree (page 19) or create a large Succulent Driftwood Centerpiece (page 25) filled with unique sealike plants! This section is full of designs and inspirations that can be elaborated into other grand statement pieces. All of these statement pieces can be exhibited on an outdoor patio or entryway or perhaps given as a gift!

SUCCULENT DRIFTWOOD TREE

Succulent driftwood trees are tall, bold and beautiful! Make this as large as you would like, creating a life-size tree planted with succulents. I collected various sizes of driftwood, arranged them in order of smallest to largest, mounted them on a piece of cedar tree and then planted a variety of succulents along the pieces of driftwood. The tree can be any shape and displays perfectly in an entryway or other location with covered light.

Supplies

- 8 pieces of driftwood in various sizes, depending on how you would like your tree shaped
- Water-sealing spray paint
- Large slab of cedar or another wood of your choice (available at lumberyards and online)
- Screws and drill (2 screws per piece of driftwood; screws need to be longer than the width of the driftwood to safely secure the wood onto the slab)
- Hot glue gun and glue sticks
- Large bag of natural sheet moss
- Gardening shears (as needed)

Plants

- 1 (4" [10-cm]) pot Echeveria 'Afterglow'
- 2 (4" [10-cm]) pots Pachyveria 'Scheideckeri'
- 3 (4" [10-cm]) pots Graptoveria 'Debbie'
- 3 (4" [10-cm]) pots Echeveria 'Neon Breaker'
- 4 (4" [10-cm]) pots Echeveria 'Perle Von Nürnberg' ('PVN')
- 2 (4" [10-cm]) pots Echeveria 'Dusty Rose'
- 2 (4" [10-cm]) pots Echeveria 'Galaxy Blue'
- 14 (4" [10-cm]) pots Othonna capensis 'Ruby Necklace'
- 1 (4" [10-cm]) pot Graptoveria 'Jules'
- 2 (4" [10-cm]) pots Graptoveria 'Opalina'
- 1 (4" [10-cm]) pot Echeveria 'Blue'
- 3 (4" [10-cm]) pots Echeveria 'Violet Queen' (with multiple heads)
- 1 (4" [10-cm]) pot Echeveria 'Elegans'
- 3 (4" [10-cm]) pots Aeonium 'Mardi Gras'

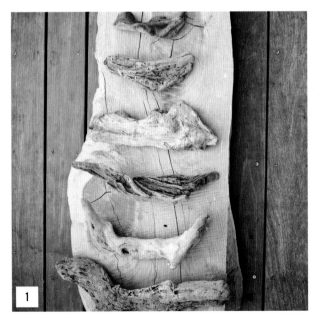

1

Craft and Arrange

1. Generously spray each driftwood piece with water-sealing spray paint. This is to ensure that the wood will not rot away from watering the succulents. Arrange the various driftwood pieces on the cedar slab. I chose to work smallest to largest, with the largest at the bottom. Once you have determined the location of the driftwood, use the drill to securely screw each piece to the cedar slab.

2. Next, remove all soil from the succulents. Starting with the bottom piece of driftwood and working left to right, attach 1 Echeveria 'Afterglow'. To attach each succulent, simply add hot glue in the location, apply moss on top of the glue, then add additional hot glue to the moss and place the succulent stem on the hot glue. Quickly add additional hot glue on top of the stem and cover with more moss. Ensure each succulent is firmly attached to the wood; if there are any loose, add a second layer of glue. If there are certain pockets in the driftwood that the succulents can nestle into, adding cactus soil is an option if they are deep enough.

3. To the right of the 'Afterglow', attach 1 *Pachyveria* 'Scheideckeri', 1 *Graptoveria* 'Debbie' and 1 *Echeveria* 'Neon Breaker'. Continue with 1 *Echeveria* 'PVN', 1 *Echeveria* 'Dusty Rose' and 1 *Echeveria* 'Galaxy Blue'. Below these, on the same piece of driftwood, fill the length with *Othonna capensis* 'Ruby Necklace' cascading over the front of the driftwood.

4. Moving up to the next (second from bottom) piece of driftwood, attach 1 *Graptoveria* 'Jules', 1 *Graptoveria* 'Opalina', 1 *Echeveria* 'Galaxy Blue' and 1 *Echeveria* 'Blue'. Underneath all of these succulents, add 'Ruby Necklace' cascading over the edges of the driftwood.

5. Moving up to the next (third from bottom) piece of driftwood, add 1 'Opalina', 1 *Echeveria* 'Violet Queen', 1 'PVN' and 1 'Neon Breaker'. If there are any open spaces, fill them with any small heads of these succulents. Then add 'Ruby Necklace' cascading over the front of the driftwood.

6. Moving up to the next (fourth from bottom) piece of driftwood, add 1 'Debbie', 1 'Scheideckeri' and 1 'Debbie'. Then add 'Ruby Necklace' cascading over the front of the driftwood.

7. Moving up to the next (fifth from bottom) piece of driftwood, add 1 small head of 'Violet Queen', 1 *Echeveria* 'Elegans', 1 small head of 'Scheideckeri' and 1 'PVN'. Then add 'Ruby Necklace' cascading over the front of the driftwood.

8. Moving up to the next (sixth from bottom) piece of driftwood, add 1 small head of 'Violet Queen', 1 'Neon Breaker', 1 'Dusty Rose' and 1 small head of 'Violet Queen'. Then add 'Ruby Necklace' cascading over the front of the driftwood.

9. Moving up to the next (seventh from bottom) piece of driftwood, add 1 small head of 'Violet Queen', 1 'PVN' and 1 small head of 'Violet Queen'. Then add 'Ruby Necklace' cascading over the front of the driftwood.

10. To finish the arrangement, attach 3 *Aeonium* 'Mardi Gras' to the top piece of driftwood.

Care

Mist each piece of driftwood with water once a week.

SUCCULENT WALL

Covering a two-story wall in succulents is probably the biggest succulent project I have done to date, and it's a major statement piece! Succulent walls can be as small or large as you would like to make them. Succulent walls thrive outside in locations with bright light. If you want to display a plant wall inside, I suggest using tropical plants or sansevierias.

For this arrangement, I used WallyGro Eco Planters, which are self-watering. Choosing the right containers for this project will set you up for a successful succulent wall.

Supplies

- 4 self-watering, hanging containers (I use WallyGro Eco Planters)
- Cactus soil

Plants

- 2 (6" [15-cm]) pots *Echeveria* 'Elegans'
- 1 (6" [15-cm]) pot *Echeveria* 'Blue Atoll'
- 2 (4" [10-cm]) pots *Sedum clavatum*
- 2 (4" [10-cm]) hanging pots *Sedum* 'Donkey Tail'
- 1 (1-gal [4-L]) pot *Xerosicyos danguyi* 'String of Coins'
- 1 (1-gal [4-L]) pot *Cotyledon* 'Chalk Fingers'
- 2 (4" [10-cm]) pots *Echeveria* 'Afterglow'
- 1 (4" [10-cm]) pot *Graptoveria* 'Debbie'
- 1 (4" [10-cm]) pot *Echeveria* 'Perle Von Nürnberg' ('PVN')
- 1 (1-gal [4-L]) pot *Senecio jacobsenii* 'Trailing Jade'
- 1 (1-gal [4-L]) pot *Echeveria* 'Sahara'
- 3 (1-gal [4-L]) pots *Oscularia deltoides*
- 2 (4" [10-cm]) pots *Echeveria* 'Blue Sky'
- 2 (4" [10-cm]) pots *Graptosedum* 'Blue Giant Hybrid' (with at least two heads)
- 1 (6" [15-cm]) pot *Echeveria* 'Blue Bird'
- 1 (4" [10-cm]) pot *Echeveria* 'Blue Sky Ruffle Hybrid'
- 1 (4" [10-cm]) pot *Echeveria* 'Rosea'

Craft and Arrange

1. First, decide where you would like to plant your succulent wall. This project's arrangement uses succulents that thrive in lots of light. Avoid succulents that have been greenhouse grown, as the leaves will quickly become sunburned in full-sun environments.

2. Fill each planter one-third of the way with soil. For this project, two planters are filled with blue succulents, one with purple succulents and one with light green succulents. In the light green planter, start with the 2 *Echeveria* 'Elegans' on either side of the planter. In the middle, place 1 *Echeveria* 'Blue Atoll', followed by both pots of the *Sedum clavatum* clusters all around the 'Blue Atoll'. In front of both 'Elegans', plant 1 pot of *Sedum* 'Donkey Tail', cascading over the front of the planter. In the middle of the planter, add the *Xerosicyos danguyi* 'String of Coins', filling in any empty spaces.

Stylish Succulent Designs & Other Botanical Crafts

3. For the purple planter, start by filling the back section with *Cotyledon* 'Chalk Fingers'. In front of the 'Chalk Fingers', add an *Echeveria* 'Afterglow' on either side of the planter, followed by the *Graptoveria* 'Debbie' and *Echeveria* 'PVN' in the center. In the front of the planter, add *Senecio jacobsenii* 'Trailing Jade' trailing over the front.

4. Start the first of the blue planters by planting the *Echeveria* 'Sahara' in the center, followed by 1 pot of *Oscularia deltoides* on either side. In the front of the planter, plant 1 *Echeveria* 'Blue Sky' on one side, then 1 pot of *Graptosedum* 'Blue Giant Hybrid', followed by an additional 'Blue Sky'.

5. For the second blue planter, start by adding 1 pot of *Oscularia deltoides* along the back of the planter. In front, add the *Echeveria* 'Blue Bird' in the center. Separate 1 pot of *Graptosedum* 'Blue Giant Hybrid' into 2 clusters and add them to either side of the 'Blue Bird'. To the left, add the *Echeveria* 'Blue Sky Ruffle Hybrid', and to the right side of the 'Blue Bird', add the *Echeveria* 'Rosea'.

Care

These specific planting containers are self-watering, meaning they have a specially designed section that blocks off the back quarter of the planter, where the water is placed. The water slowly filtrates through the planter, watering all the succulents. With these planters, the water compartment needs to be filled only twice a month or, if the succulents seem dry, once a week.

Note: Try planting various types of plants to cover different walls. Shaded walls are the perfect home for tropical plants!

SUCCULENT DRIFTWOOD CENTERPIECE

This natural piece of driftwood is filled with sealike succulents, creating a large centerpiece that looks as if it just came from the ocean! This specific driftwood piece was about 3 feet (91 cm) in length, which made for the perfect grand centerpiece display. The succulents are essentially planted in moss on top of the driftwood, so weekly misting is all that is needed to care for this arrangement!

Supplies

- Water-sealing spray paint
- Large piece of driftwood (available at floral supply stores, craft stores or online)
- Hot glue gun and glue sticks
- Large bag of natural sheet moss

Plants

- 1 (6" [15-cm]) pot *Echeveria* 'Dusty Rose'
- 2 (6" [15-cm]) pots *Echeveria* 'Neon Breaker'
- 1 (6" [15-cm]) pot *Echeveria* 'Pink Ruffle Hybrid'
- 1 (6" [15-cm]) pot *Echeveria* 'Lilacina'
- 1 (6" [15-cm]) pot *Echeveria* 'Afterglow'
- 1 (4" [10-cm]) pot *Echeveria* 'Blue Galaxy'
- 1 (4" [10-cm]) pot *Echeveria* 'Lilacina'
- 1 (4" [10-cm]) pot *Graptoveria* 'Debbie'
- 2 (4" [10-cm]) pots *Pachyveria* 'Blue Mist'
- 1 (4" [10-cm]) pot *Echeveria* 'Rosea'
- 2 (4" [10-cm]) pots *Echeveria* 'Raindrops'
- 1 (4" [10-cm]) pot *Echeveria* 'Perle Von Nürnberg' ('PVN')
- 1 (4" [10-cm]) pot *Echeveria* 'Violet Queen'
- 1 (2" [5-cm]) pot *Graptosedum* 'California Sunset'

Craft and Arrange

1. Generously spray the entire driftwood piece with water-sealing spray paint. This is to ensure that the wood will not rot away from watering the succulents. Next, remove all soil from the succulents.

1

3a

3b

2. Plan the location of each succulent. Since each driftwood piece will vary, I suggest creating clusters of succulents and placing them around the driftwood or keeping all of the succulents together to create one large design, which is what I did here. For my driftwood piece, I decided to make three rows of colorful succulents. To recreate this design, you may need to use additional or fewer succulents depending on the size and shape of your driftwood piece.

3. In the top row, working from left to right, attach 1 *Echeveria* 'Dusty Rose' and 1 *Echeveria* 'Neon Breaker', followed by the *Echeveria* 'Pink Ruffle Hybrid', then the additional 'Neon Breaker'. Next, attach the 6-inch (15-cm) *Echeveria* 'Lilacina' and the *Echeveria* 'Afterglow' to finish off this row. To attach the succulents to the driftwood, add hot glue to the driftwood, then quickly add a small clump of sheet moss. Then, add hot glue on top of the moss, add the succulent stem to the hot glue and quickly add another layer of hot glue and moss. In this project, you are essentially planting the succulents in moss on the driftwood, securing them with glue. If the succulents are loose to the touch, add additional glue to help them adhere.

4. Underneath this top row, working from left to right, attach the *Echeveria* 'Blue Galaxy', then the 4-inch (10-cm) *Echeveria* 'Lilacina', followed by the *Graptoveria* 'Debbie'. Next, add both *Pachyveria* 'Blue Mist' side by side. In the bottom row, start with the *Echeveria* 'Rosea', then *Echeveria* 'Raindrops', *Echeveria* 'PVN' and *Echeveria* 'Violet Queen'. On the end of this row, add an additional 'Raindrops'.

5. To finish the arrangement, add the *Graptosedum* 'California Sunset' under the second 'Neon Breaker'.

Care

Mist the succulent clusters with water twice a week. As the succulents start to grow over time, snip off the ends and replant the succulents back onto the driftwood or in soil!

SUCCULENT-FILLED TABLE

Succulent-filled tables are major backyard envy pieces and are so simple to make! Take an old table and re-create it into a dreamy succulent masterpiece. This project has colorful and flashy succulents lining the center of a wooden table. This makes the perfect outdoor patio decoration and counter for entertaining, leaving your guests impressed!

Supplies

- Wooden table
- Saw or multi-tool, for cutting out table's center
- Wooden planter box (choose one that will fit in the center of the table, or plan to construct one that is attached in the center)
- Nails (optional)
- Wood stain and paintbrush (optional)
- Cactus soil

Plants

- 1 (6" [15-cm]) pot *Echeveria* 'Cassyz Winter'
- 2 (6" [15-cm]) pots *Graptopetalum superbum* (with at least 2 heads)
- 2 (6" [15-cm]) pots *Echeveria* 'Elegans'
- 2 (6" [15-cm]) pots *Graptoveria* 'Opalina'
- 2 (6" [15-cm]) pots *Echeveria* 'Blue Bird'
- 2 (6" [15-cm]) pots *Echeveria* 'Neon Breaker'
- 1 (6" [15-cm]) pot *Echeveria* 'Violet Queen'
- 2 (6" [15-cm]) pots *Echeveria* 'Subsessilis'
- 1 (6" [15-cm]) pot *Echeveria* 'Perle Von Nürnberg' ('PVN')
- 1 (6" [15-cm]) pot *Echeveria* 'Ruffles'
- 1 (6" [15-cm]) pot *Echeveria* 'Blue Curls'

Craft and Arrange

1. For this project, I used a table that had a premade planter box in the center. You can ask your local woodsmith to create one for you, too—however, crafting your own is easy! First, cut out the center section of the table you plan to plant in. I chose to have the succulents planted in the center, but other designs can be done using the same method. Next, measure the empty space to add a planter box to fit in the section. The planter box can rest in the empty space to keep it removable, or you can attach it more permanently with nails. Once the table is crafted, you can leave it natural or stain the wood a color you like. When you are finished crafting the table, fill the planter halfway with soil.

2. Start by planting the *Echeveria* 'Cassyz Winter' in one end of the planter, with 1 *Graptopetalum superbum* at its side. Behind them, plant 1 *Echeveria* 'Elegans' and 1 *Graptoveria* 'Opalina'. Next, plant 1 *Echeveria* 'Blue Bird' and 1 *Graptopetalum superbum*, then 1 *Echeveria* 'Neon Breaker' and the *Echeveria* 'Violet Queen'. Then plant 1 *Echeveria* 'Subsessilis' with 1 *Graptopetalum superbum*, and follow with the *Echeveria* 'PVN' and the *Echeveria* 'Ruffles'. Now, plant the *Echeveria* 'Blue Curls', the remaining 'Opalina', then the remaining *Graptopetalum superbum*. Lastly, plant the remaining 'Blue Bird' and the second 'Neon Breaker', then the second 'Elegans' and the second 'Subsessilis'.

Care

Gently water the planter once a week. I recommend using either a garden squeeze bottle or a light setting on a garden hose. If the succulents appear dry, water them more frequently. If they grow out of the table over time, snip off the excess length and plant them back in the table's soil or in an additional planter.

2b

SUCCULENT FOUNTAIN

Succulent fountains are lush, elaborate and bountiful, and they have quickly become one of my favorite projects. Taking an old and rundown fountain and transforming it into a large, succulent-filled statement piece is sure to set you apart in the neighborhood! In this project, plant the succulents directly into the fountain where water would traditionally go, creating an illusion of flowing "water" with cascading succulents! This project is ideal for a fountain that does not work any longer, but of course can be made from any fountain. When designing your succulent fountain, be sure to determine where you would like to display your piece, then choose succulents accordingly. The succulents in the following plant list do best in partial-sun environments.

Supplies

- Large fountain (I used one with 3 tiers that measured 54" [137 cm] tall)
- Cactus soil

Plants

- 3 (6" [15-cm]) pots *Echeveria* 'Princess Lace'
- 6 (6" [15-cm]) pots *Echeveria* 'Afterglow'
- 5 (6" [15-cm]) pots *Echeveria* 'Cassyz Winter'
- 6 (6" [15-cm]) pots *Echeveria* 'Neon Breaker'
- 1 (1-gal [4-L]) pot *Echeveria* 'Purple Pearl'
- 4 (6" [15-cm]) pots *Echeveria* 'Blue Sky'
- 6 (4" [10-cm]) pots *Senecio* 'String of Pearls'
- 4 (4" [10-cm]) pots *Sedum* 'Donkey Tail'
- 4 (6" [15-cm]) hanging pots *Peperomia* 'Ruby Cascade'
- 6 (6" [15-cm]) hanging pots *Cotyledon pendens* 'Cliff Cotyledon'

Craft and Arrange

1. Clear any debris from the fountain, then fill the fountain tiers three-quarters full with soil. I used a three-tiered fountain for this project.

2

2. Starting in the middle tier and working left to right, plant 1 *Echeveria* 'Princess Lace', then 1 *Echeveria* 'Afterglow', followed by 1 *Echeveria* 'Cassyz Winter'. Next comes 1 *Echeveria* 'Neon Breaker', another 'Cassyz Winter', then another 'Afterglow', finishing the row with 1 'Neon Breaker'.

3. Next, in the top tier, plant the *Echeveria* 'Purple Pearl' in the center, facing upward, then plant 1 'Neon Breaker' directly in front of the 'Purple Pearl'. To the right side of the 'Neon Breaker', plant 1 *Echeveria* 'Blue Sky', followed by 1 *Echeveria* 'Afterglow' in the corner of the top tier. On the left side of the 'Neon Breaker', plant 1 'Afterglow' in the other corner.

4. In the bottom tier, start by planting 1 'Neon Breaker' and then 1 'Cassyz Winter' and 1 'Afterglow'. The next section will have 2 rows of succulents. Begin by planting the bottom layer from left to right with 1 'Blue Sky', 1 'Neon Breaker', another 'Blue Sky' and then another 'Neon Breaker'. Above this layer, plant 1 'Princess Lace', 1 'Cassyz Winter', the remaining 'Princess Lace' and 1 additional 'Cassyz Winter'. After this double layer, plant 1 'Afterglow' and finish with the remaining 'Blue Sky'.

5. The last part of this arrangement is to fill trailing succulents over all of the edges. To plant the trailing succulents, it is easiest to bare-root (remove the soil from) all the heads of succulents and plant the heads individually. In the top tier, underneath the far-left 'Afterglow', plant 2 pots of *Senecio* 'String of Pearls'. On either side of the 'Neon Breaker', plant 2 pots of *Sedum* 'Donkey Tail'. Underneath the 'Neon Breaker', plant 2 pots of 'String of Pearls'. Underneath the last 'Afterglow', plant the remaining 2 pots of 'String of Pearls'. In the middle tier, plant the 4 pots of *Peperomia* 'Ruby Cascade' under all the succulents. On the bottom tier, plant the 6 pots of *Cotyledon pendens* 'Cliff Cotyledon'.

Care

Gently water the fountain once a week. If the succulents look dry, gently water twice a week. Since fountains usually have some type of drainage, draining excess water can be easily done.

5

SUCCULENT BIRDBATH

Decorative birdbaths make superb planters for succulents, creating an exquisite living statement piece. The succulents will be planted where the birds once splashed around. In this arrangement, I used a variety of cascading and trailing succulents around the edges of the birdbath, and filled the center with large, vibrant succulents. All of these plants thrive in full-sun environments, so be sure to choose the birdbath's location accordingly.

Supplies

- Empty birdbath (I used a birdbath that was 30" [76 cm] tall and 22" [56 cm] wide on the top)
- Clear, water-sealing spray paint, to refurbish the birdbath (optional)
- Cactus soil

Plants

- 2 (8" [20.5-cm]) pots *Sedum* 'Donkey Tail' (with long trailing heads)
- 4 (6" [15-cm]) pots *Senecio jacobsenii* 'Trailing Jade'
- 2 (1-gal [3.8-L]) pots *Echeveria* 'Andromeda'
- 2 (1-gal [3.8-L]) pots *Echeveria* 'Misty Lilac'
- 2 (1-gal [3.8-L]) pots *Graptoveria* 'Platinum'
- 2 (1-gal [3.8-L]) pots *Echeveria* 'Hawaii'
- 2 (1-gal [3.8-L]) pots *Echeveria* 'Sahara'
- 4 (1-gal [3.8-L]) pots *Graptosedum* 'Blue Giant Hybrid'
- 4 (1-gal [3.8-L]) pots *Crassula platyphylla variegata*

Craft and Arrange

1. Spray paint the birdbath, if necessary. I recommend using a clear, water-sealing spray paint. Next, fill the birdbath halfway with soil.

2

2. Separate all the multiheaded succulents. Around the edges of the birdbath, plant groupings of 10 to 12 heads of *Sedum* 'Donkey Tail', then groupings of 6 to 8 heads of *Senecio jacobsenii* 'Trailing Jade', alternating between them until the entire edge of the birdbath is planted.

3. Next, on top of the trailing succulents, working from left to right, plant 1 *Echeveria* 'Andromeda', then 1 *Echeveria* 'Misty Lilac', followed by 1 *Graptoveria* 'Platinum'. Moving to the right, plant 1 *Echeveria* 'Hawaii', and then the remaining 'Misty Lilac'. Plant the remaining 'Andromeda', followed by the remaining 'Platinum', finishing with the remaining 'Hawaii'. In the center of the birdbath, plant the 2 *Echeveria* 'Saharas' next to each other. In any empty spaces, plant *Graptosedum* 'Blue Giant Hybrid' and *Crassula platyphylla variegata* heads, filling the entire birdbath with succulents.

Care

Gently water the succulent birdbath once a week. Since there aren't any drainage holes, light watering is essential so the succulents do not flood. Drilling holes in the bottom of the birdbath is also an option. If, during the warmer months, the succulents are drying out quickly, adjust to water more often.

3

EVENTS & WEDDINGS

Wow your guests next time you entertain with perfectly arranged Succulent Planter Box Centerpieces (page 47), and leave them with a lasting impression with effortless Succulent Favors (page 43). Or enhance your wedding with handcrafted Succulent Boutonnieres (page 39) and Moss Baskets (page 49). Succulents make exceptional, longer-lasting alternatives to fresh florals, so they can be enjoyed after the event is over. In most projects, they can be deconstructed from the arrangement and planted in soil to keep living! Creating living accents for your event or wedding adds a special touch, and just wait until guests find out you did it yourself!

SUCCULENT BOUTONNIERES

From weddings to school dances to formal affairs, succulent boutonnieres make the perfect accessory to any men's attire. These easy-to-make boutonnieres can be enjoyed long past the one-night event by planting the succulent after! Years down the road, when all you have to remember the event by are photos and memories, your succulent can thrive into a large plant of its own, as a sweet reminder!

Supplies

- Small bucket of water
- Paper or cloth towel
- Thick floral wire
- Wire cutters
- Green floral tape
- Strong glue (optional)
- White satin adhesive ribbon (or add a drop of glue to regular ribbon)
- Boutonniere pin

Plants

- 1 (2" [5-cm]) pot *Echeveria* 'Blue Prince'
- Small sprig of *Eucalyptus*
- Small cluster of *Hydrangea* 'White'

Craft and Arrange

1. Remove all soil and roots from the succulent, leaving just the stem. Next, rinse the stem with water to remove any extra soil, then gently dry it off with the towel. Using the floral wire, gently puncture the wire through the center of the stem, underneath the bottom leaf of the succulent, pulling it through to create a loop. Snip off any excess wire that is longer than 3 inches (7.5 cm) on each side.

1a

1b

1c

2a

2b

3a

3b

2. Next, starting underneath the succulent's bottom leaves, start wrapping floral tape down the wire. To wrap the tape, firmly twist the tape around the wire, wrapping the tape on top of the tape from the previous wrap, leaving the wire completely wrapped. Next, add the sprigs of *Eucalyptus* and *Hydrangea*. Position the stem next to the succulent, placing them on top of the floral tape. Wrap the stems of the *Eucalyptus* and *Hydrangea* into the boutonniere, starting at the top of the arrangement and moving downward, just like wrapping the succulent.

3. To finish off the boutonniere, starting at the bottom of the wire, wrap the adhesive floral ribbon upward to the bottom of the arrangement. Tie a tight knot in the back of the arrangement to secure the arrangement, then snip off the back of the ribbon. To attach the boutonniere to clothing, simply use a boutonniere pin and poke it through the ribbon, underneath the bottom leaves of the succulents.

Care

These specific boutonnieres thrive best if made the night before the event, due to the fresh *Hydrangea*. If using just *Eucalyptus* and succulents, making these up to 3 days prior is possible. Simply mist the succulent with 1 or 2 sprays of water the night before the event to keep the leaves perky.

When finished using the boutonniere, carefully peel off the ribbon and tape layers from the arrangement, remove the wire and plant the succulent stem in soil. The succulent will continue to blossom.

Note: Boutonnieres can be made with a variety of succulents and floral combinations, selected and positioned as you wish. *Echeverias* are the most ideal succulent to use in this craft due to their structure and hardiness. Try using colored ribbon to match different dress colors.

SUCCULENT FAVORS

Succulent favors make the perfect takeaway from weddings, parties or your next event. With endless color options, succulent combinations, various vessels and containers to choose from, succulent favors can be customized in every way! Using succulent favors at your next event is sure to impress the crowd and lets them take home a part of the event! Try displaying your favors in a fun holder (page 45) or with tags like "party!" (page 44).

Supplies

- 16 mini votive candle holders
- 1 large bag forest green reindeer moss
- 1 large bag light green reindeer moss
- 1 chopstick
- 1 small package green preserved Spanish moss
- 1 small package tan preserved Spanish moss
- Cupcake toppers or picks (optional)

Plants

- 4 (2" [5-cm]) pots *Echeveria* 'Elegans'
- 4 (2" [5-cm]) pots *Echeveria* 'Prolifica'
- 4 (2" [5-cm]) pots *Echeveria* 'Neon Breaker'
- 4 (2" [5-cm]) pots *Echeveria* 'Lilacina'

Craft and Arrange

1. Fill each votive to the top with one type of reindeer moss. Using a chopstick, poke a hole in the middle of the moss, creating space to plant the succulents. Next, gently remove the soil from the succulent, leaving the roots. Position the roots in the space created in the moss. The moss will be surrounding the succulent, so from the outside, it will look like all moss.

2. Using the chopstick, slightly snuggle the succulent in the moss, making sure it is secure. Then, place a small amount of Spanish moss under the bottom leaves of the succulent, using the chopstick to tuck it in, creating a fluffy texture around the top of the votive.

3. Repeat these steps for all the votives, using 1 succulent per votive and mixing various moss colors! While planting the favors, pair darker green mosses with the lighter hues of *Echeveria* 'Elegans' and *Echeveria* 'Prolifica'. Lighter-colored mosses complement the dark colors of *Echeveria* 'Neon Breaker'; tan moss goes well with *Echeveria* 'Lilacina.'

Care

Mist the succulents twice a week with a small amount of water. The specific succulents used in this project thrive best with indirect light. Heavy full sun can cause sunburnt leaves.

Note: Mini votive holders are commonly sold in the candle or wedding sections of craft stores.

A combination of various mosses, rocks, shells, sands, glasses, and so on can be added at the bottom of the votive to create a different accent look! Also, try adding a cupcake topper or pick!

SUCCULENT PLANTER BOX CENTERPIECE

Succulent planter box centerpieces are the perfect decor! Designed with low-growing succulents, these centerpieces are easy to talk over. Filling these long planter boxes with flower-like succulents adds a floral ambience to an event in place of fresh florals that will be tossed afterward. Succulent planter box centerpieces can be utilized at an event, then transitioned onto a home dining room table where the succulents can continue to flourish.

Supplies

- Wood stain or paint and paintbrush
- Wooden planter box (36" [91.5 cm] long x 4" [10 cm] wide x 4" [10 cm] tall)
- Protective furniture sliders/feet, for underneath box
- Plastic sheeting, to line the box
- Staple gun
- Cactus soil

Plants

- 1 (6" [15-cm]) pot Echeveria 'Blue Curls'
- 2 (4" [10-cm]) pots Echeveria 'Subsessilis'
- 4 (4" [10-cm]) pots Sedum 'Donkey Tail'
- 2 (4" [10-cm]) pots Echeveria 'Rosea'
- 2 (6" [15-cm]) pots Echeveria 'Violet Queen'
- 2 (4" [10-cm]) pots Echeveria imbricata 'Blue Rose'
- 2 (4" [10-cm]) pots Echeveria 'Perle Von Nürnberg' ('PVN')
- 2 (4" [10-cm]) pots Echeveria 'Lola'
- 2 (6" [15-cm]) pots Echeveria 'Blue Sky'

Craft and Arrange

1. Start by staining or painting the wooden box (I chose a brown stain to make the succulents stand out). Next, push the protective sliders onto the underside of the box on all 4 corners. Now, line the inside of the box with plastic, using a staple gun to attach it. Fill the planter box one-quarter of the way with soil.

2. Working from the center of the box outward, plant the Echeveria 'Blue Curls' in the center, followed by 1 Echeveria 'Subsessilis', angled, on each side of it; then 1 pot of Sedum 'Donkey Tail', equally separated into 2 portions, on each side, flowing over the sides of the box. Next to the 'Donkey Tail', add 1 Echeveria 'Rosea' on each side, then diagonally, add an Echeveria 'Violet Queen' on each side of the planter next to the 'Rosea'.

3. Diagonal to the 'Violet Queen', add an Echeveria imbricata 'Blue Rose' on each side, then an Echeveria 'PVN' on each side. Plant a pot of 'Donkey Tail' next to the right and left of the 'PVN' on either side of the planter box. Next, add an Echeveria 'Lola' to either side of the planter box, followed by the last pot of 'Donkey Tail', equally separated into 2 clusters, on each side. Finish the arrangement with a large Echeveria 'Blue Sky' on each end.

Care

Mist the succulents twice a week with a small amount of water. If the planter box will generally be kept inside, place the planter box outside for an afternoon sun once per week. This will refresh the succulent's natural colors. The plastic on the inside of the planter will help prevent leaking when watering it, and the protective sliders will help prevent the box from scratching the surface of your table. If you plan to keep the box outside, the succulents will thrive in a covered area, out of direct sunlight.

SUCCULENT "FLOWER" MOSS BASKET

Succulent "flower" baskets are the perfect accessory for any flower girl, and they also make a classy decoration or present. With lush and flowerlike succulents planted into the basket, this is an arrangement that will keep living long after the event!

Supplies

- Small moss basket (can be lined with plastic or unlined)
- Cactus soil
- Small gardening spade

Plants

- 1 (4" [10-cm]) pot *Echeveria imbricata* 'Blue Rose'
- 1 (2" [5-cm]) pot *Echeveria* 'Neon Breaker'
- 1 (2" [5-cm]) pot *Pachyveria* 'Powder Puff'
- 1 (4" [10-cm]) pot *Echeveria* 'Dusty Rose'
- 1 (2" [5-cm]) pot *Graptopetalum paraguayense* 'Ghost Plant'
- 1 (2" [5-cm]) pot *Sedeveria* 'Blue Elf'
- 1 (2" [5-cm]) pot *Echeveria* 'Painted Lady'

Craft and Arrange

1. Fill the moss basket halfway with soil. Starting at one end of the basket, plant the *Echeveria imbricata* 'Blue Rose'. Next, plant the *Echeveria* 'Neon Breaker' and *Pachyveria* 'Powder Puff'. Add the *Echeveria* 'Dusty Rose' in the middle of the basket, followed by the *Graptopetalum paraguayense* 'Ghost Plant'. Finish by adding the *Sedeveria* 'Blue Elf' and then the *Echeveria* 'Painted Lady' on the far end.

Care

Gently mist the succulent-filled basket twice a week. Since the basket is shallow, gentle misting will ensure that your arrangement does not get flooded.

1

SUCCULENT LETTER

Succulent-filled wooden letters make perfect arrangements to display at an event or wedding, which can then be added to your home as living decor! Try adding a succulent letter to a display table at a wedding, spell out fun expressions, such as LOVE, or gift someone with their family initial. The number of succulents you'll need to use will depend on the letter you choose. In this arrangement, I chose to make the letter "C" for my last name, Cain. If you're not up for crafting your own letter planter, you can find them online or ask your local woodsmith to make you one.

Supplies

- Wood boards, plywood and wood glue or wooden letter planter (I used one 14" [35.5 cm] tall x 2½" [6.5 cm] deep)
- Frame backing (optional)
- Wood stain and paintbrush
- Hot glue gun and glue sticks
- Large bag of natural sheet moss
- Chopstick or garden scissors (optional)

Plants

- 1 (4" [10-cm]) pot *Graptoveria* 'Blue Pearl' (with at least 3 heads)
- 2 (4" [10-cm]) pots *Echeveria* 'Perle Von Nürnberg' ('PVN')
- 1 (4" [10-cm]) pot *Echeveria* 'Neon Breaker'
- 2 (2" [5-cm]) pots *Echeveria* 'Painted Lady'
- 1 (4" [10-cm]) pot *Echeveria* 'Violet Queen'
- 1 (4" [10-cm]) pot *Echeveria* 'Blue Curls'
- 1 (2" [5-cm]) pot *Graptosedum* 'California Sunset'

Craft and Arrange

1. To make the wooden letter, use wood glue to attach 1 x 2-inch (2.5 x 5-cm) pieces of wood board to form the edges of the letter of your choice. Use ½-inch (1.3-cm) plywood to form the back, using wood glue to attach the wood boards to the plywood. If using a frame backing, attach it now. Some letters hang best with two backings.

2. Next, stain the wooden letter. While it is drying, remove all soil from the succulents. If the succulents have excess soil, cut the roots and soil off to create succulent cuttings.

1

3. Starting in one corner of the letter, attach one cutting of *Graptoveria* 'Blue Pearl'. Do this by adding hot glue on the stem of the succulent, followed by a clump of natural sheet moss, adhering the cutting to the inside of the letter. Add additional glue and moss to secure it if the succulent cutting seems loose.

4. Continuing with this method, attach 1 *Echeveria* 'PVN', followed by the *Echeveria* 'Neon Breaker' and 1 *Echeveria* 'Painted Lady'. Then add 1 cutting of 'Blue Pearl' and the *Echeveria* 'Violet Queen'. Now, add the additional 'PVN', then *Echeveria* 'Blue Curls'. Follow with the second 'Painted Lady', a cutting of 'Blue Pearl' and *Graptosedum* 'California Sunset'. Attaching the last succulent can easily be done by using a chopstick or the edge of garden scissors, securing it in place.

Care

Mist the letter twice a week. The succulents will start to root in the moss inside of the letter. Once the succulents outgrow the letter (6 to 8 months), clip the succulents, and either reattach them to the letter with shorter stems, or plant them in soil and watch them grow.

Note Try spelling out a fun word or adding two initials with an ampersand (&) in between!

Feeling BEACHY

Down by the beach is always my favorite place to be! Bring part of the beachy spirit home with beautiful tillandsia and succulent arrangements. These beach-inspired crafts make the perfect addition to a beach house, vacation home or coastal-decorated house! Fill large conch shells with trailing succulents (page 57) or make a living Tillandsia Grapewood Centerpiece (page 65) that is simply elegant to display anywhere. You'll love finding fun places to hang Succulent Orbs (page 71), or dangle a large *Tillandsia* driftwood mobile filled with "jellyfish" (page 67). Whether you are a regular beachcomber or a tropical vacationer, this chapter will inspire a beach-themed crafting obsession!

SUCCULENT SHELLS

Collecting shells has always been a hobby of mine, but what I enjoy more is finding unique ways to display them. Planting succulents inside shells is a beautiful way to add a creative accent piece to your home and showcase the elegance of the shell paired with the living greenery.

Supplies

- 1 large pink conch shell (8" to 9" [20.5 to 23 cm] long)
- Cactus soil
- Chopsticks or small gardening spade

Plants

- 3 (4" [10-cm]) pots *Sedum* 'Donkey Tail' (cuttings will also work)

Craft and Arrange

1. Remove the succulents from their growing pots and separate the multiple heads, categorizing them from small to large. Determine how you would like to display the shell, and then place soil in the opening of the shell, filling it about two-thirds full.

2

2. At the bottom of the shell, begin planting the largest *Sedum* 'Donkey Tail' heads. Tuck the bottom of the roots inside the shell, nudging the base of the roots with a chopstick or small gardening spade to secure them inside the shell. Continue to plant each head of 'Donkey Tail', working with the largest to the smallest heads from the bottom to the top of the shell.

3. Once the shell is filled, gently poke the chopstick in between the heads to ensure they are securely planted in the shell. Lightly misting the soil can help with this.

Care

Mist the succulents twice a week. 'Donkey Tail' thrives best in bright light habitats, but the leaves can get sunburned in direct harsh light. If you choose to display your succulent shell inside, simply place the arrangement in a location with bright light or bring it outside once a week for the afternoon sun to refresh the succulents' natural color.

Note: Try arranging succulents in smaller shells. To get the succulents to stay in a smaller shell, use a variety of succulent cuttings, attach preserved sheet moss inside of the shells with hot glue and then hot glue the cuttings with the sheet moss. Mist twice a week with water.

In small pink murex shells (shown on the opposite page), I used 1 cutting each of *Crassula platyphylla variegata*, *Oscularia deltoides* and *Anacampseros telephiastrum variegata* 'Sunrise'.

In the small black murex shells, I used 2 small cuttings of *Sedum* 'Donkey Tail' and 1 cutting each of *Corpuscularia lehmannii* 'Ice Plant', *Senecio* 'Narrow Leaf Chalksticks' and *Senecio serpens* 'Blue Chalksticks'.

3

TILLANDSIA JELLYFISH URCHIN VASE

Inspired by the swift and delicate jellyfish in the Caribbean, this eye-catching air plant display re-creates a "swimming" jellyfish by pairing a living *Tillandsia* and a sea urchin shell. The urchin represents the jellyfish body, and the air plant acts as the tentacles. Make sure your sea star, urchins and shell will fit easily inside the vase you use.

Supplies

- Thin fishing line
- Scissors
- 1 large sea urchin shell (slightly smaller than the opening of the vase)
- E6000 industrial adhesive glue
- 1 (5" [12.5-cm])-long branch of natural cholla wood
- 1 small sea urchin shell
- Glass cylindrical vase (mine was 12" [30.5 cm] tall x 4" [10 cm] wide)
- 2 oz (55 g) blue mixed aquarium gravel
- 1 small sea star
- 1 small decorative shell

Plants

- 1 *Tillandsia caput-medusae* (air plant)
- 1 *Tillandsia ionantha fuego* (air plant)

Craft and Arrange

1. Cut a 24-inch (61-cm)-long piece of fishing line and loop it around the bottom tentacles of the *Tillandsia caput-medusae*, double-knotting it. Next, slide the top of the fishing line through the bottom of the large urchin, continuing on through the opening at the top. The air plant will be hanging out of the urchin, with its tentacles facing downward. Using the E6000, add glue around the bottom opening of the urchin, then quickly attach the bottom of the air plant to the glue, holding for 2 to 3 minutes, or until adhered and dry.

Stylish Succulent Designs & Other Botanical Crafts

4a

4b

2. Next, tie the top of the fishing line (with the air plant urchin hanging down) to the cholla wood, double-knotting it to secure it. The top of the urchin should be dangling 1 to 2 inches (2.5 to 5 cm) from the cholla wood.

3. To arrange the small urchin, add E6000 glue around the opening of the small urchin, then quickly attach the *Tillandsia ionantha fuego*, facing upward, to the glue. Hold the air plant and urchin shell together for 2 to 3 minutes to adhere and let the glue dry.

4. Place the aquarium gravel in the bottom of the vase. Next, add the small air plant urchin, with the tentacles facing upward. Beside the small urchin, position the small sea star and decorative shell. Then, slowly guide the dangling air plant urchin inside the vase, resting the cholla wood on top of the vase.

Care

Air plants thrive in low or indirect light and should be misted twice a week. For this arrangement, it is easier to take out the urchins to mist them, which also prevents water stains inside the glass.

TILLANDSIA GRAPEWOOD CENTERPIECE

With this centerpiece, *Tillandsias* are fabulously displayed on a bed of moss inside of a grapewood trunk. Best of all, the centerpiece can be re-created into another arrangement without detaching plants. Impress your guests with this sophisticated and unique centerpiece!

Supplies

- 1 grapewood trunk (about 10" [25.5 cm] long) (You can find grapewood in the beach or wood section of craft stores.)
- Medium bag of green preserved Spanish moss
- Medium bag of green preserved reindeer moss

Plants

- 1 medium *Tillandsia xerographica*
- 2 small *Tillandsia brachycaulos*
- 2 medium *Tillandsia aeranthos* 'Purple Fan'
- 2 small *Tillandsia velickiana*

Craft and Arrange

1. Place a combination of the Spanish moss and reindeer moss inside the grapewood trunk. The moss mixture should sit on top of the trunk. Gently nudge it into any crevices or tight spaces.

2a

2b

2. In the middle of the trunk, plant the *Tillandsia xerographica*, softly wrapping the curly tentacles around the edges of the trunk. On either side of the *xerographica*, add 1 *Tillandsia brachycaulos*, nestling its bottom on top of the moss. Next, add a *Tillandsia aeranthos* 'Purple Fan' on either side of the *brachycaulos*. Finish with 1 *Tillandsia velickiana* on either end. The air plants will rest above the moss on the trunk. To change up the arrangement, simply place the air plants in different locations.

Care

Tillandsias are unique plants that live in the air without any soil at all. To care for these unique creatures, mist them twice a week. *Tillandsias* do not like direct sunlight and thrive in low-light locations.

Note Air plants can be added on top of any surface! Try adding an air plant on top of a large wood stump covered in moss to create fun accent decor!

TILLANDSIA JELLYFISH MOBILE

Tillandsia jellyfish, dangling along a piece of driftwood, makes for an appealing accent piece! This project brings back the ever-popular mobile craft in a living way. Hang the jellyfish mobile against a wall to add texture and design, or dangle it in a playroom or nursery!

Supplies

- Thin fishing line
- Scissors
- 5 large sea urchin shells (3" to 4" [7.5 to 10 cm] wide)
- E6000 industrial adhesive glue
- Large, thin piece of driftwood (about 30" [76 cm] long, 2" to 3" [5 to 7.5 cm] wide)
- 2 sturdy nails, for hanging

Plants

- 1 large blooming *Tillandsia caput-medusae* (4" to 8" [10 to 20.5 cm] long)
- 2 large *Tillandsia butzii* (about 8" [20.5 cm] long)
- 2 large *Tillandsia caput-medusae* (4" to 8" [10 to 20.5 cm] long)

Craft and Arrange

1. Cut a 24-inch (61-cm)-long piece of fishing line. Wrap the fishing line around the bottom 3 or 4 tentacles of a *Tillandsia caput-medusae*, double-knotting it. Next, slide the top of the fishing line through the bottom of a sea urchin, continuing on through the opening on the top. The air plant will be hanging out of the urchin, with its tentacles facing downward.

2. To attach the air plant to the shell, use the E6000 to glue around the bottom opening of the urchin and attach the bottom of the air plant to the glue, holding for 2 to 3 minutes until adhered and dry. Continue this method for all 5 *Tillandsias* and urchin shells, using a new piece of fishing line each time.

1a

3. Take a piece of fishing line and the jellyfish urchin and tie it onto the left end of the driftwood, so that the jellyfish dangles about 16 inches (40.5 cm) below, double-knotting it to secure.

4. Repeat the process with 1 *Tillandsia butzii* jellyfish–urchin, dangling about 10 inches (25.5 cm) below the driftwood. Continue alternating between *butzii* and the other *caput-medusae,* until all the jellyfish–urchins have been used, evenly spreading out the *Tillandsias* over the length of the driftwood. To hang this arrangement, use 2 sturdy nails for it to rest on, letting the *Tillandsias* dangle down.

Care

Air plants thrive in low or indirect light and should be misted twice a week.

Note: Also try hanging a single air plant jellyfish from a tree during the holidays!

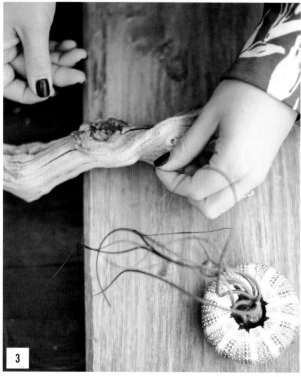

SUCCULENT ORB

Orbs have an elegant, natural aesthetic, and filling them with colorful succulents takes simple twine to the next level! These living succulent orbs make the perfect hanging accessory for a patio umbrella or tree, or they can be placed on a shelf or a table. You can find orbs for purchase online or in craft stores—they're often in the coastal decor section.

Supplies

- 1 (10" [25.5-cm]) twine orb, available online and at craft stores
- Hot glue gun and glue sticks
- 1 small bag natural sheet moss
- Twine, to hang the orb

Plants

- 1 (4" [10-cm]) pot Echeveria 'Raindrops'
- 1 (4" [10-cm]) pot Echeveria 'Afterglow'
- 1 (4" [10-cm]) pot Echeveria 'Lola'
- 4 cuttings of Ceropegia woodii 'String of Hearts'

Craft and Arrange

1. Remove all soil from the succulents, leaving just the stems. Add a thin layer of moss onto the bottom of the twine orb. To do this, add hot glue, then quickly cover with moss.

2. Begin by adding the Echeveria 'Raindrops' on the far left. Attach the succulent on top of the moss with hot glue, quickly covering the stem and hot glue with additional moss. Then, attach the Echeveria 'Afterglow' in the center, followed by the Echeveria 'Lola' on the right edge. Next, add 1 cutting of Ceropegia woodii 'String of Hearts' on either side of the 'Raindrops'. Then, add 1 cutting of 'String of Hearts' on either side of the 'Lola'. Finish off the arrangement by tying a piece of twine on top of the orb to hang it.

Care

Lightly mist the succulents twice a week.

1

Seasonal FESTIVITIES

Living plant art can be enjoyed for each season—even winter, believe it or not! Holidays are always a time for people to come together, so try adding festive DIY crafting to your seasonal celebrations for a unique and special touch. Try a living Succulent Pumpkin Centerpiece (page 75) that can last from September to December, or celebrate summer with a patriotic Succulent USA Flag Planter (page 99). February is the month of love, so show some succulent love with Succulent Heart Boxes (page 83). Any season is perfect for a succulent wreath! Learn how to make both hand-glued and hand-wired Succulent Wreaths (pages 89 and 93). Whichever holidays you celebrate, get festive by making your own plant art!

SUCCULENT PUMPKIN CENTERPIECE

Succulent pumpkins are the perfect fall craft, and they're also what kicked off my entire succulent business! These centerpieces were first created by the talented designer Laura Eubanks of Design for Serenity, and they were then popularized by author Debra Lee Baldwin. This arrangement will last for two to three months and can be planted after pumpkin season is over! These make one-of-a-kind Thanksgiving centerpieces or host gifts. The same method for making succulent pumpkins can be done on other fall squash or faux pumpkins.

Supplies

- Spray adhesive glue
- Large Princess/Fairytale pumpkin, uncarved
- Latex gloves
- Medium bag of brown preserved Spanish moss
- Hot glue gun and glue sticks, or white glue
- Decorative moss (optional)

Plants

- 1 (6" [15-cm]) pot *Echeveria* 'Cassyz Winter'
- 1 (6" [15-cm]) pot *Echeveria* 'Subsessilis'
- 1 (4" [10-cm]) pot *Echeveria* 'Neon Breaker' (with 2 heads)
- 1 (4" [10-cm]) pot *Echeveria* 'Misty Lilac'
- 2 (4" [10-cm]) pots *Echeveria imbricata* 'Blue Rose'
- 1 (4" [10-cm]) pot *Echeveria* 'Raindrops'
- 1 (4" [10-cm]) pot *Echeveria* 'Cassyz Winter'
- 1 (6" [15-cm]) pot *Corpuscularia lehmannii* 'Ice Plant'
- 1 (4" [10-cm]) pot *Kalanchoe fedtschenkoi variegata*
- 2 (4" [10-cm]) pots *Senecio* 'String of Pearls' (full of long strands)
- 1 (4" [10-cm]) pot *Sedum* 'Donkey Tail' (full of multiple heads)

Craft and Arrange

1. Using the spray glue, lightly spray the top third of the pumpkin, then quickly add a ½-inch (1.3-cm)-thick layer of Spanish moss on top of the glue. I recommend wearing latex gloves during this process, as the spray adhesive glue is extremely sticky. Reinforce the moss with either hot glue or white glue if there are any loose areas. Having the moss securely anchored to the pumpkin is crucial, because this is where the succulents will start to root.

2. Remove all soil from the succulents, leaving just the stems. If there are too many roots or the soil is too messy to work with, simply cut the roots and soil off, leaving just the stem. Now you're ready to start arranging your succulents.

1a

Stylish Succulent Designs & Other Botanical Crafts

3. For this arrangement, *Corpuscularia lehmannii* 'Ice Plant' and *Kalanchoe fedtschenkoi variegata* succulents work perfectly as fillers, *Senecio* 'String of Pearls' and *Sedum* 'Donkey Tail' dangle over the edges of the pumpkin and bright-colored *Echeverias* star in the center of the arrangement. Place 1 large *Echeveria* 'Cassyz Winter', 1 large *Echeveria* 'Subsessilis', 1 double-headed *Echeveria* 'Neon Breaker' and 1 *Echeveria* 'Misty Lilac' in the center of the pumpkin. Since purple pairs well with orange, I suggest adding larger purple succulents toward the center of the pumpkin, so they stand out.

4. Take the end of each succulent stem and place it on top of the moss. Add hot or white glue under the stem and above the stem of the succulent. Then, quickly cover the glue with additional moss. If the succulents are still loose, add more glue and moss. It is crucial that the succulents are securely attached to the pumpkin. (Hot glue is easier to use for this project as it dries more quickly.)

5. Using the same method and working outward from the center, add 2 *Echeveria imbricata* 'Blue Rose', 1 *Echeveria* 'Raindrops' and 1 small *Echeveria* 'Cassyz Winter'. Position these succulents alongside the larger succulents in the center. In between these, fill any empty spaces with 'Ice Plant' and *Kalanchoe fedtschenkoi variegata*.

6. Finally, use 'String of Pearls' and 'Donkey Tail' to wrap the edges of the arrangement with cascading succulents. Alternate between the 2 succulents, with small clusters of both. If you'd like, add decorative moss in between the succulents to add pops of color or accents, or to fill empty spaces. Add glue to attach the moss to desired locations.

Care

Mist twice a week with water. The succulents will start to root in the moss. If the succulents become loose while living on the pumpkin, add additional glue to secure them. Once the season for your pumpkin is over, the succulents can be replanted in 2 ways. The first method is by pulling each succulent cutting off the pumpkin, then planting it in soil. The second method is by slicing the top third of the pumpkin off. Once it is sliced, plant the pumpkin top with succulents still attached in soil. The pumpkin will decompose and the succulents will continue to grow.

Note. Try using a white pumpkin for this project! For the white pumpkins, I suggest using purple, orange and green succulents. *Sedum* 'Donkey Tail' also works well for cascading down the sides of the pumpkin. These could be paired with *Senecio* 'String of Pearls' or by themselves. *Echeveria* 'Topsy Turvy' pairs well with *Echeveria* 'Violet Queen' as the center, with fillers of *Sedum reflexum* and *Sedum* 'Brown Beans' surrounding the *Echeverias*.

SUCCULENT MINI PUMPKINS

Mini succulent pumpkins are wonderful for all things fall and harvest related. These make the perfect gifts, Thanksgiving place card holders, festive party favors or accent decor! Try arranging the succulents on a variety of colored pumpkins for a unique look!

Supplies

- 3 mini pumpkins, uncarved (striped, orange, white, etc.)
- Spray adhesive glue
- Green or brown preserved sheet moss
- Latex gloves
- Hot glue gun and glue sticks, or white glue

Plants for White Mini Pumpkins

- 1 cutting of *Graptosedum* 'California Sunset'
- 1 cutting of *Sedum* 'Pink Jelly Beans'
- 1 cutting of *Portulacaria afra variegata* 'Rainbow Bush'
- 2 cuttings of *Sedum reflexum*
- 2 cuttings of *Sedum confusum*

Plants for Striped Mini Pumpkins

- 1 cutting of *Graptosedum* 'California Sunset'
- 1 cutting of *Aeonium* 'Kiwi'
- 1 cutting of *Echeveria harmsii* 'Ruby Slippers'
- 1 cutting of *Oscularia deltoides*
- 2 cuttings of *Sedum* 'Pink Jelly Beans'

Plants for Orange Mini Pumpkins

- 1 cutting of *Sedum* 'Pink Jelly Beans'
- 1 cutting of *Aeonium* 'Kiwi'
- 1 cutting of *Sedum clavatum*
- 2 cuttings of *Oscularia deltoides*

Craft and Arrange

1. Starting with the white pumpkin, lightly spray the top quarter of the pumpkin with spray glue, then quickly add a ¼-inch (6-mm)-thick layer of sheet moss on top of the glue. You may choose to wear latex gloves for this process. Reinforce the moss with either hot glue or white glue if there are any loose areas.

2. Arrange the cuttings of *Graptosedum* 'California Sunset', *Sedum* 'Pink Jelly Beans', *Portulacaria afra variegata* 'Rainbow Bush', *Sedum reflexum* and *Sedum confusum* on top of the white pumpkin, so the colors alternate between green and pink, with a variety of yellow and blue accent colors. Take the end of each succulent stem and place it on top of the moss. Next, add hot or white glue under the stem and above the stem of the succulent, then quickly cover the glue with sheet moss. Use the same method for all the succulent cuttings, adhering them to the pumpkin one at a time.

1a

1b

2b

2a

3

4

3. Moving to the striped pumpkin, attach the moss with the spray glue, using the same method as you did with the white pumpkin. Arrange the cuttings of *Graptosedum* 'California Sunset', *Aeonium* 'Kiwi', *Echeveria harmsii* 'Ruby Slippers', *Oscularia deltoides* and *Sedum* 'Pink Jelly Beans' on top of the striped pumpkin, so that the colors are alternating between red, green and blue. Attach the succulents to the moss with the hot glue or white glue.

4. Moving to the orange pumpkin, attach the moss with the spray glue. Arrange the cuttings of *Sedum* 'Pink Jelly Beans', *Aeonium* 'Kiwi', *Sedum clavatum* and *Oscularia deltoides* on top of the orange pumpkin, so the colors alternate between blue and green, with a pop of pink accenting. Attach the succulents to the moss with the hot glue or white glue.

Care

Mist twice a week. The succulents will start to root in the moss. If the succulents become loose while living on the pumpkin, add additional glue to secure them. Once the season for your pumpkin is over, the succulents can be replanted in two ways. The first method is by pulling each succulent cutting off the pumpkin, then planting them in soil. The second method is by slicing the top third of the pumpkin off. Once it is sliced, plant the pumpkin top with succulents still attached in soil. The pumpkin will decompose and the succulents will continue to grow.

Note: Try adding a hand-stamped name card or "Thankful" tag to the pumpkin. Simply glue a corner of the card or tag onto part of the pumpkin or hole-punch a corner of the card and tie a twine bow, then glue!

SUCCULENT HEART BOX

Succulent-filled heart boxes make an excellent gift to express your love, or perhaps you can show some self-love and make one to keep! Filled with Valentine's Day colors, this heart box is the ideal gift that will flourish beyond any fresh floral arrangement.

Supplies

- Wood boards, plywood and wood glue or a wooden heart box (6" x 6" [15 x 15 cm], 2½" [6.5 cm] deep)
- Wood stain or paint and paintbrush
- Frame backing (optional)
- Hot glue gun and glue sticks
- Small bag of gray or brown preserved Spanish moss
- Chopsticks or garden scissors (optional)

Plants

- 1 (4" [10-cm]) pot *Crassula platyphylla variegata*
- 2 (2" [5-cm]) pots *Anacampseros telephiastrum variegata* 'Sunrise'
- 2 (2" [5-cm]) pots *Echeveria* 'Perle Von Nürnberg' ('PVN')
- 2 (2" [5-cm]) pots *Pachyphytum oviferum* 'Pink Moonstone'
- 2 (2" [5-cm]) pots *Echeveria* 'Cubic Frost'
- 1 (4" [10-cm]) pot *Echeveria harmsii* 'Ruby Slippers'
- 1 (2" [5-cm]) pot *Graptoveria* 'Blue Pearl'

Craft and Arrange

1. To make a wooden heart box, use wood glue to attach various pieces of 1 x 2-inch (2.5 x 5-cm) wood board to form the edges of the heart. Use ½-inch (1.3-cm) plywood to form the back, using wood glue to attach the wood boards to the plywood. Stain or paint the wooden heart box, and add the frame backing once it's dry. You can also use a premade heart-shaped wooden box. If you can't find one, try reaching out to a local woodsmith with a photo of what you want.

2. While the box is drying, remove all soil from the succulents. If the succulents have excess soil, cut off the roots and soil. Beginning in a corner of the heart, place 1 cutting of *Crassula platyphylla variegata* in the heart box. Add hot glue on the stem of the succulent, followed by some Spanish moss, adhering the cutting to the inside of the box. Add additional glue and moss if the succulent cutting seems loose, securing the succulent.

2a

2b

3. Continuing with the same method, follow with 1 cutting each of *Anacampseros telephiastrum variegata* 'Sunrise', *Echeveria* 'PVN' and *Pachyphytum oviferum* 'Pink Moonstone', working toward the center of the heart. Next, continuing downward in the heart box, add *Echeveria* 'Cubic Frost', 2 cuttings of *Echeveria harmsii* 'Ruby Slippers' and 1 cutting of 'PVN'. Progressing upward, add *Graptoveria* 'Blue Pearl', then 'Ruby Slippers', 2 cuttings of 'Sunrise', 1 of 'Pink Moonstone', and 1 of *Crassula platyphylla variegata*. Fill any remaining space with extra cuttings. Attaching the last succulent can easily be done by using a chopstick or the edge of garden scissors, securing it in place.

Care

Mist the heart twice a week. The succulents will start to root in the moss inside of the heart. Once the succulents outgrow the heart (4 to 5 months), clip the succulents and either reattach them to the heart box with shorter stems, or plant them in soil and watch them blossom.

SUCCULENT HANGING PINECONES

When I was younger, I always found it exciting to treasure hunt for large pinecones, but I never knew what to do with them. Making succulent pinecones is the perfect way to transform and display them as living art. In this project, add succulents to the base of the pinecone, creating succulent arrangements that can be used as ornaments for a tree, hanging accessories outside or handmade gifts!

Supplies

- Twine
- Scissors
- Hot glue gun and glue sticks
- Large pinecone (6" to 7" [15 to 18 cm] tall) (I used Giant Sugar Pinecones)
- Spray adhesive glue
- Small bag of green preserved sheet moss

Plants

- 1 (2" [5-cm]) pot *Anacampseros rufescens*
- 1 (4" [10-cm]) pot *Crassula rubricaulis* 'Candy Cane'
- 1 (4" [10-cm]) pot *Crassula pubescens radicans* 'Cranberry Crumbles'
- 1 (4" [10-cm]) pot *Crassula rupestris*
- 1 (6" [15-cm]) pot *Peperomia* 'Ruby Cascade'

Craft and Arrange

1. Cut a 14-inch (35.5-cm) piece of twine. Tie a bow near the ends of the twine, creating a large opening. Take the centermost part of the twine loop opposite to the bow knot and hot glue it to the flattened bottom of the pinecone. Then, using the spray glue, lightly spray the rest of the flattened bottom of the pinecone and quickly add sheet moss to cover. Add reinforcement under the moss with hot glue if there are any loose areas.

2. Remove all soil from the succulents, leaving just the ends behind. Starting in the center of the pinecone and avoiding adding any glue to the loose twine, add hot glue to a small section of pinecone. Place 1 *Anacampseros rufescens* cutting on top of the glue, add extra hot glue, then quickly cover with sheet moss, adding pressure on top of the cutting to adhere it to the pinecone.

1a

1b

2a

2b

3. Working outward from the center and continuing with the same method, attach a cluster of *Crassula rubricaulis* 'Candy Cane' on each side of the *Anacampseros rufescens*. Directly behind the *Anacampseros rufescens*, attach a cluster of *Crassula pubescens radicans* 'Cranberry Crumbles'. Next to this, add a *Crassula rupestris* cutting on each side. Next, on the edges of the pinecone, add strands of *Peperomia* 'Ruby Cascade' flowing down the sides of the pinecone. Hang the pinecone with the twine for display.

Care

Mist twice a week. The succulents will start to root in the moss. After the season is over, or if you would like to repurpose the succulents, snip the cuttings off the pinecone, and then replant, or use them to make a different arrangement.

SUCCULENT WREATH (GLUED)

Succulent wreaths can be enjoyed any time of the year! For spring, light pastel-colored succulents can be refreshed on the succulent wreath, whereas warm-colored succulents can be replenished for fall. For the festive holiday season, add a sparkly bow on top and you can enjoy a living succulent wreath all year long!

Supplies

- 1 (14" [35.5-cm]) round grapevine wreath
- Spray adhesive glue
- Large bag of green or brown preserved sheet moss
- Hot glue gun and glue sticks
- Bow for the top (optional)

Plants

- 1 (4" [10-cm]) pot *Echeveria* 'Raindrops'
- 1 (4" [10-cm]) pot *Echeveria* 'Dusty Rose'
- 1 (4" [10-cm]) pot *Echeveria* 'Perle Von Nürnberg' ('PVN')
- 2 (4" [10-cm]) pots *Echeveria* 'Pulidonis'
- 5 (2" [5-cm]) pots *Graptoveria* 'Jules'
- 4 (4" [10-cm]) pots *Sedum clavatum*
- 2 (2" [5-cm]) pots *Echeveria* 'Violet Queen'
- 2 (4" [10-cm]) pots *Echeveria* 'Afterglow'

Craft and Arrange

1. Spray the bottom half of the wreath with spray adhesive glue, then quickly add sheet moss on top of the glue. Add reinforcement under the moss with hot glue if there are any loose areas. Having the moss securely attached to the wreath is crucial.

2. Remove all soil from the succulents, leaving just the stem. If there are too many roots or the soil is too messy to work with, simply cut off the roots and soil, leaving just the stem. Place 1 *Echeveria* 'Raindrops' in the center of the wreath, add hot glue, then place the succulent on top. Add additional glue on top of the succulent stem and quickly cover with moss, adding slight pressure on the succulent to secure it to the wreath. If the succulent still seems loose, add another layer of glue with moss.

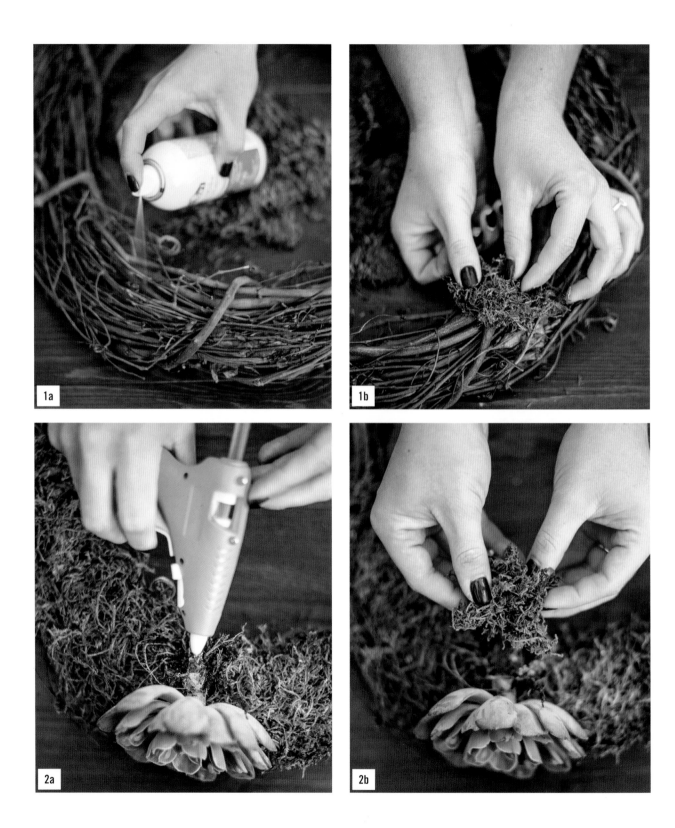

3. Keep adding succulents, using the same method, covering the bottom half of the wreath with succulents. Attach 1 *Echeveria* 'Dusty Rose' to the left and 1 *Echeveria* 'PVN' to the right of the 'Raindrops'. Next, attach an *Echeveria* 'Pulidonis' on each side. Underneath the 'Raindrops', add 1 *Graptoveria* 'Jules', followed by 1 pot of *Sedum clavatum* on each side of the 'Jules'. Underneath the 'Dusty Rose' and the 'PVN', add 1 'Jules'. Next, add a cluster of *Sedum clavatum* on either side, followed by an *Echeveria* 'Violet Queen' on either side as well. To finish the wreath, add 1 'Jules' on each side of the 'Violet Queen', followed by the 2 *Echeveria* 'Afterglow' standing tall at the top of each side. If using a bow, hot glue the bow on top of the wreath.

Care

Mist the bottom half of the wreath, where the succulents are, twice a week. The succulents will start to root in the moss on the wreath. Once the succulents outgrow the wreath (5 to 7 months), clip the succulents and either reattach them to the wreath with shorter stems or plant them in soil and watch them grow.

Note: Try adding succulents all around the circumference of the wreath (as shown on the right). To do this, simply glue succulents on the wreath until there aren't any open spaces!

SUCCULENT WREATH (HAND WIRED)

Hand wiring succulents onto a wreath form is an art in itself. In this project, each succulent gets hand wired into the moss. Craft your own wreath by learning this technique, and watch the succulents grow into the moss of the wreath!

Supplies

- Large bag of natural sphagnum moss
- Bin of water
- Latex gloves (optional)
- 1 (10" [25.5-cm]) round metal wreath form
- Green floral wire
- Wire clippers
- Floral pins (optional, needed only for extra-large succulents)
- Gardening shears

Plants

- 3 (4" [10-cm]) pots *Graptoveria* 'Fred Ives'
- 2 (4" [10-cm]) pots *Echeveria* 'Lilacina'
- 2 (4" [10-cm]) pots *Echeveria* 'Sanyatwe'
- 2 (4" [10-cm]) pots *Echeveria* 'Neon Breaker'
- 1 (4" [10-cm]) pot *Echeveria* 'Royalty Hercules'
- 2 (4" [10-cm]) pots *Echeveria* 'Perle Von Nürnberg' ('PVN')
- 1 (4" [10-cm]) pot *Echeveria* 'Rosea'

Craft and Arrange

1. Remove all the soil from the succulents, leaving just the stem or bare roots. Soak the sphagnum moss in the bin of water, then ring out the excess water (you may choose to wear latex gloves for this). Add the sphagnum moss all around the front of the wreath form. Wrap floral wire several times around one end of the metal form, almost as if you were tying a knot with the wire, then twist to secure it to the form. With the wire still attached, wrap it around the moss along the circumference of the wreath form, leaving about two fingers' worth of width between each wrap, so that all the moss is securely attached to the wreath.

2. With the wire still attached from wrapping the moss, place the bottom of 1 *Graptoveria* 'Fred Ives' stem on top of the moss-covered wreath and wrap the wire around the stem about four times. Then, add a small chunk of moss on top of the stem and secure the succulent by wrapping the bottom part with wire another 4 to 6 times, just as you attached the wire to the wreath.

3. Using the same method and moving from right to left, attach 1 *Echeveria* 'Lilacina'. Next, attach 1 *Echeveria* 'Sanyatwe', 1 *Echeveria* 'Neon Breaker' and the *Echeveria* 'Royalty Hercules'. Now, attach 1 'Fred Ives', 1 *Echeveria* 'PVN' and the *Echeveria* 'Rosea'. This should put you halfway through the wreath. Continue with the last 'Fred Ives', the remaining 'Sanyatwe' and the remaining 'Lilacina'. Finish with the remaining 'Neon Breaker', followed by the remaining 'PVN'. If there are particularly large succulent stems, push a floral pin into the moss to help secure it, then add wire wrapping.

4a

4. To finish the wreath, cut the wire with about 10 inches (26 cm) to spare and wrap that piece of wire around itself to form a knot. Add two knots on top of these to secure, then cut away the loose ends.

Care

Water the succulent wreath gently once a week. Misting twice a week is also an option. As the succulents grow, soaking the base of the wreath in water for 15 minutes once a week is also a great alternative.

Hand-wired succulent wreaths will last about 6 to 8 months before the succulents start to grow out. As the succulents grow, snip the elongated succulents and rewire them back into the wreath. The succulents can also be planted in soil after they outgrow the wreath.

Note: If the succulents being used do not have long stems, use a floral pin to poke through the base of the succulent (see photo 3). Then, poke the floral pin into the moss, wrap the floral wire around the floral pin and succulent about eight times and continue the crafting method.

4b

SUCCULENT TABLETOP TREE

Layered with festively colored red and green succulents and topped with a gold "star," this succulent Christmas tree makes the perfect complement to holiday decor! After the holiday season, deconstruct the succulents and create a whole new arrangement!

Supplies

- Medium bag of Royal Pool moss
- 1 (16" [40.5-cm] tall) grapevine tree
- Spray adhesive glue
- Latex gloves (optional)
- Large bag of natural sheet moss
- Hot glue and glue sticks, or white glue

Plants

- 8 (1-gal [4-L]) pots *Echeveria harmsii* 'Ruby Slippers'
- 5 (1-gal [4-L]) pots *Sedum* 'Aurora'
- 8 (4" [10-cm]) pots *Sedum clavatum*
- 4 (1-gal [4-L]) pots *Graptopetalum paraguayense* 'Ghost Plant'
- 8 (4" [10-cm]) pots *Crassula ovata* 'Dwarf Jade Plant'
- 3 (4" [10-cm]) pots *Aeonium* 'Emerald Ice'

Craft

1. Place the Royal Pool moss inside the grapevine tree, with smaller chunks in the top and larger chunks at the base of the tree. Next, using the spray adhesive glue, spray the entire outside of the tree, then quickly cover with a thin layer of sheet moss. Add reinforcement under the moss with either hot glue or white glue if there are any loose areas.

2. Begin by separating all stems of the multiheaded succulents. Starting at the bottom of the tree and moving upward diagonally, attach 1 *Echeveria harmsii* 'Ruby Slippers'. To do this, take the end of the stem and place it on top of the moss. Next, add hot glue under and above the stem of the succulent, then quickly cover the glue with sheet moss. Use the same method for all the succulent cuttings, adhering them to the grapevine tree.

2a

2b

3

4

3. Using the same method and continuing upward in a diagonal direction, make a path of *Sedum* 'Aurora' all the way to the top of the tree, wrapping the path around the width. Next, attach *Sedum clavatum* above the 'Aurora', all around the tree, following the same diagonal pattern to the top of the tree. Above the *Sedum clavatum*, attach a row of *Graptopetalum paraguayense* 'Ghost Plant'. Below the initial row of 'Ruby Slippers', add a row of *Crassula ovata* 'Dwarf Jade Plant' and then another row of 'Aurora', filling in any empty spaces.

4. On top of the tree, attach the *Aeonium* 'Emerald Ice' to represent a star. Attach all 3 next to each other, filling in the entire top.

Care

Gently mist twice a week. If planning to keep the tree beyond the holidays, when the succulents start to grow out, snip the stems and reattach them to the tree. If planning to deconstruct the tree after the holidays, snip off all the succulent cuttings and plant them in a new arrangement, a decorative pot or your garden. Try saving the grapevine tree for next year, and you can replant it again!

SUCCULENT USA FLAG PLANTER

Inspired by my mother's strawberry, blueberry and whipped cream Fourth of July cake, I decided to make a living American flag using succulents! Combining red, white and blue naturally colored succulents, this flag is a festive way to celebrate the USA. Showcase your patriotism with this colorful planter for Memorial Day, the Fourth of July, Veteran's Day or any other patriotic occasion!

Supplies

- Rust-Oleum clear glossy spray, to prevent rusting
- Large metal planter (20" [51 cm] long x 14" [35.5 cm] wide x 4" [10 cm] tall)
- Cactus soil
- Chopsticks or small garden shovel, for arranging

Plants

- 12 (2" [5-cm]) pots *Echeveria* 'Blue Hybrid'
- 1 (6" [15-cm]) pot *Sedum* 'Cape Blanco'
- 6 (1-gal [4-L]) pots *Crassula platyphylla*
- 20 (2" [5-cm]) pots *Echeveria* 'White'

Craft and Arrange

1. Spray Rust-Oleum all around the metal planter, then let it dry for about 30 minutes. Next, fill the planter halfway with soil. Now you are ready to arrange the succulents in the pattern of a flag!

2. Starting with the top left corner, plant 4 *Echeveria* 'Blue Hybrid', adding small clusters of *Sedum* 'Cape Blanco' in between them. Using a chopstick to help plant the succulents tightly together is helpful. Underneath this row, add 2 more rows of the same pattern of 4 'Blue Hybrid', with clusters of 'Cape Blanco' between. This creates the stars and blue section of the flag.

3. Now, on to the "red and white" stripes. To the top row of the planter, add 1 pot of *Crassula platyphylla*, planting a thin line along the top. Underneath, add 6 *Echeveria* 'White', planting them as closely as you can. Underneath this row, add another row of *Crassula platyphylla*, followed by 6 more *Echeveria* 'White'. Next comes the first full row of *Crassula platyphylla*—plant these up against the bottom of the *Echeveria* 'White' and 'Blue Hybrid', creating a row the entire length of the planter. Under this row, add the last 8 *Echeveria* 'White', followed by a final row of *Crassula platyphylla*, completing the USA flag design.

Care

Lightly mist the flag planter twice a week. These succulents thrive best outside in indirect light.

Outdoor DECOR

Outdoor gardens and patios can be filled with lush botanicals and colorful plants. In this chapter, learn to make arrangements to accent your outdoor space, complement your garden, or add a special touch to your patio! Craft a Succulent Pot in a Pot (page 105) that has cascading succulents or make Tillandsia Dangling Spheres (page 107) to hang from your trees! Arrange your own Fuzzy Succulent Garden (page 111), full of all fuzzy and soft succulents, or try a Succulent Ombré Pastel Planter (page 113) that makes the perfect patio table centerpiece. Oftentimes, a covered outdoor space with bright light is the perfect habitat for succulents to thrive in. I encourage creativity in this section, as these are ideas your imagination can run with!

SUCCULENT POT IN A POT

Inspired by the trendy #succiepotinapot on social media, planting a smaller-sized pot inside a larger pot creates a one-of-a-kind arrangement. This planter has bright and colorful succulents in the center and succulents cascading down. The design is the perfect centerpiece for an outdoor patio!

Supplies

- 1 (10" [25.5-cm]) terra-cotta pot
- Cactus soil
- 1 (6" [15-cm]) terra-cotta pot
- Chopstick or small garden shovel
- Pumice

Plants

- 1 (4" [10-cm]) pot *Graptoveria* 'Opalina'
- 1 (4" [10-cm]) pot *Pachyveria* 'Blue Mist'
- 1 (4" [10-cm]) pot *Crassula perforata variegata*
- 1 (4" [10-cm]) pot *Othonna capensis* 'Ruby Necklace'

Craft and Arrange

1. Start with the largest pot, and fill it three-quarters full with soil. Create a small hole in the middle to place the smaller pot on top of the soil, lying flat sideways. Add soil inside the opening of the smaller pot. Now you are ready to arrange and plant with succulents.

1a

1b

2a

2b

2. Plant the *Graptoveria* 'Opalina' and the *Pachyveria* 'Blue Mist' side by side in the smaller pot that is nestled into the larger pot. If needed, tuck any loose roots into the smaller pot by using a chopstick or small shovel. Next, separate the heads of *Crassula perforata variegata*, and gently nestle them above the 2 succulents that are already planted. Lastly, separate the various strands of *Othonna capensis* 'Ruby Necklace'. Plant all of the 'Ruby Necklace' along the edge of the smaller pot, cascading over the edge. Finish the arrangement by covering any soil showing with pumice.

Care

Gently water the succulents by misting the arrangement 1 to 2 times per week. The succulents in this arrangement have been grown in a greenhouse, meaning they thrive best in indirect light.

TILLANDSIA DANGLING SPHERES

Dangling *Tillandsia* spheres make the most dazzling outdoor garden decor! This simple yet elegant display is sure to be an eye-catching piece swinging from backyard trees. Fill various metal spheres with moss and air plants, then tie them to one another to dangle outside. These dangling spheres make great alternatives to wind chimes, accents to patio decks and overhangs or even an accessory in the garden—the options are endless!

Supplies

- Wired natural twine
- 1 large metal sphere (12" [30.5 cm])
- Wire cutters
- 1 medium metal sphere (5⅛" to 8⅛" [13 cm to 21 cm])
- 1 small metal sphere (3⅛" to 6⅛" [8 cm to 15 cm])
- Large bag of green preserved Spanish moss

Plants

- 1 large (9" [23-cm]) *Tillandsia xerographica*
- 1 medium (6" [15-cm]) *Tillandsia velickiana*
- 3 small (3" [7.5-cm]) *Tillandsia harrisii*

Craft and Arrange

1. Loop the wired twine around three of your fingers and twist it at the end, creating a hanging loop. Next, bring the twine down about 6 inches (15 cm) from the loop, take the large sphere and wrap the twine around the top of the sphere 3 or 4 times. Now, using the wire cutters, snip the twine at the bottom of the twist. At the bottom of the large sphere, attach the wired twine by twisting it around the sphere, wrapping it about 3 or 4 times. Then, bring the twine down 3 inches (7.5 cm) and attach the medium sphere, using the same method as for the large. Repeat the same steps for the small sphere, cutting the end of the twine after you are finished with each sphere.

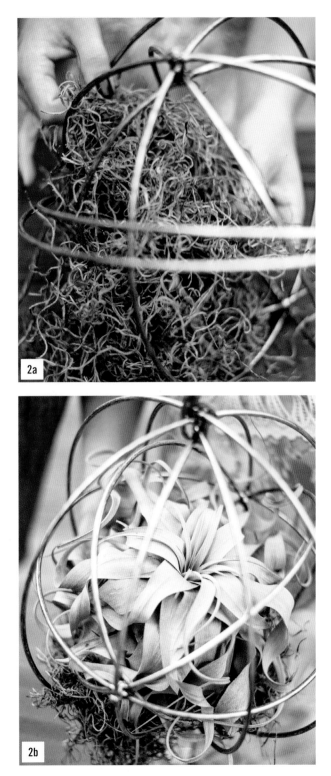

2a

2b

2. This sphere arrangement is organized from large to small as it cascades downward. In the largest sphere, add a generous handful of green Spanish moss, then top it with the large *Tillandsia xerographica*. Since *xerographicas* have plenty of curly tentacles, positon a couple around the edges of the spheres. To the medium sphere, add a moderate handful of green Spanish moss, then place the medium *Tillandsia velickiana* on top. Finally, in the small sphere, add a small handful of green Spanish moss, followed by a trio of *Tillandsia harrisii*. To arrange the trio, simply take the ends of all 3 air plants and gather them together, then place them inside the sphere.

Care

Tillandsias are air plants and thrive best in bright-light locations, but not direct sunlight. This arrangement would do best hanging from a shaded patio deck, backyard trees or any area that does not get harsh sun. To care, mist or gently water twice a week. If watering with a garden hose, adjust the setting to a light mist or light shower. If you live in a region that has cold winters, bring the arrangement inside, or the plants will freeze!

FUZZY SUCCULENT GARDEN

Growing up, I always loved gardening with different members of my family. The very first garden I can recall making was a fuzzy plant garden. This project is inspired by that childhood memory and is planted with soft, texture-filled succulents. Each one has a unique feel to the leaves, but none is thorny. This arrangement is visually appealing and fuzzy to touch!

Supplies

- 1 (12" [30.5-cm]-long) wooden planter (lined with plastic or unlined)
- Cactus soil
- Small garden shovel

Plants

- 4 (4" [10-cm]) pots *Kalanchoe tomentosa* 'Light Panda Plant' (with at least 3 heads each)
- 3 (4" [10-cm]) pots *Kalanchoe tomentosa* 'Teddy Bear' (with at least 3 heads each)
- 2 (4" [10-cm]) pots *Echeveria* 'Pulv-Oliver' (with at least 5 heads each)
- 2 (4" [10-cm]) pots *Echeveria setosa* 'Mexican Firecracker'
- 2 (4" [10-cm]) pots *Echeveria setosa variegata deminuta* 'Firecracker Plant'
- 3 (2" [5-cm]) pots *Sempervivum aracnoides*
- 2 (4" [10-cm]) pots *Kalanchoe millotii*
- 2 (4" [10-cm]) pots *Kalanchoe* 'Snow White Panda'
- 2 (4" [10-cm]) pots *Cotyledon variegata* 'Bear Paws Variegated'

Craft and Arrange

1. Fill the wooden planter three-quarters of the way with soil. Separate all the succulent heads. Take 2 heads of the *Kalanchoe tomentosa* 'Light Panda Plant' and place them in the far right back corner of the box. Next to these, add 2 heads of *Kalanchoe tomentosa* 'Teddy Bear', followed by 2 heads of 'Light Panda Plant'. Continue alternating the 'Teddy Bear' and 'Light Panda Plant' until the back row is filled. I used 4 sets of 'Teddy Bear' and 5 sets of 'Light Panda Plant'.

2. Below this row, starting on the far right, add 2 heads of *Echeveria* 'Pulv-Oliver', then 1 *Echeveria setosa* 'Mexican Firecracker' and 2 more heads of 'Pulv-Oliver'. Next, add 1 *Echeveria setosa variegata deminuta* 'Firecracker Plant', then 2 heads of 'Pulv-Oliver' and the remaining 'Mexican Firecracker'. Follow with 2 more heads of 'Pulv-Oliver', the remaining 'Firecracker Plant' and 2 more 'Pulv-Oliver' heads.

3. Underneath this row, starting on the far right, add 1 *Sempervivum aracnoides*, then 1 pot of *Kalanchoe millotii* followed by 1 pot of *Kalanchoe* 'Snow White Panda'. Then, add 1 pot of *Cotyledon variegata* 'Bear Paws Variegated', 1 *Sempervivum aracnoides* and then the remaining pot of *Kalanchoe millotii*. Add the last pot of 'Bear Paws Variegated', 'Snow White Panda' and the remaining *Sempervivum aracnoides* to finish the arrangement.

Care

All these fuzzy succulents are best kept outside in covered light, but not direct sunlight. To care, mist with water twice a week. Since this container does not have a drainage hole, be sure not to overwater the arrangement, so the succulents do not flood.

1

2

SUCCULENT OMBRÉ PASTEL PLANTER

Succulents naturally come in every color of the rainbow, which makes arranging them by color intriguing! This pastel succulent planter showcases the beauty of ombré by highlighting eight different pink and purple succulents. Try crafting a similar design with other succulent colors.

Supplies

- 1 (10" [25.5-cm]) square wooden planter box lined with plastic
- Cactus soil
- Chopsticks or small garden shovel

Plants

- 6 (2" [5-cm]) pots *Echeveria* 'Lola'
- 7 (2" [5-cm]) pots *Graptopetalum paraguayense* 'Ghost Plant'
- 7 (2" [5-cm]) pots *Pachyphytum oviferum* 'Pink Moonstone'
- 7 (2" [5-cm]) pots *Echeveria* 'Cubic Frost'
- 7 (2" [5-cm]) pots *Graptoveria* 'Debbie'
- 7 (2" [5-cm]) pots *Echeveria* 'Perle Von Nürnberg' ('PVN')
- 4 (2" [5-cm]) pots *Echeveria* 'Dusty Rose'
- 5 (2" [5-cm]) pots *Graptoveria* 'Jules'

Craft and Arrange

1. Begin by filling the planter box three-quarters of the way with soil. Plant the pots of *Echeveria* 'Lola' (the lightest-colored succulent) in the bottom corner of the planter box. Use a chopstick to help squeeze the succulents to be planted tightly together. Next, add a diagonal row with the pots of *Graptopetalum paraguayense* 'Ghost Plant', followed by a row of the 7 pots of *Pachyphytum oviferum* 'Pink Moonstones'. The pinks will now slowly start to fade into purple. Add the pots of *Echeveria* 'Cubic Frost' next, followed by the pots of *Graptoveria* 'Debbie', then the pots of *Echeveria* 'PVN'. Finish off the planter box with the darkest purples, the pots of *Echeveria* 'Dusty Rose' and, finally, the *Graptoveria* 'Jules'.

Care

This planter box thrives on a covered outdoor patio or somewhere with indirect light. Full sun is too harsh and can burn the leaves. Mist the arrangement with water 1 to 2 times per week.

Found Around
THE HOME

From old wineglasses to tired cupcake stands, outdated picture frames to empty bamboo bowls that don't serve a purpose any longer, the projects in this chapter repurpose your old household items to give them new life. Transform a cupcake stand with succulents (page 119), or convert your fruit basket into a kitchen centerpiece (page 123). Or make a picture frame into a living terrain with a Tillandsia Picture Frame (page 131). The options are endless for new vessels to plant in!

SUCCULENT CUPCAKE STAND

The details on vintage cupcake stands make them beautiful to display, and adding succulents creates a lush and green-filled piece. In this craft, transform an old cupcake stand, and plant cupcakelike succulents where the cakes once were.

Supplies

- Empty cupcake stand (I used a 2-tiered, 23-count cupcake holder)
- Scissors
- Large package of light green reindeer sheet moss
- 2 rolls of forest ribbon moss
- Hot glue gun and glue sticks
- Medium bag of green reindeer moss (same color as the moss ribbon)
- Medium bag of light green reindeer moss (same color as the reindeer sheet moss)

Plants

- 23 (2" [5-cm]) pots of cupcake-looking succulents. The variety I used in this project include:
    - *Echeveria* 'Lime N Chile'
    - *Echeveria* 'Lolita'
    - *Echeveria* 'Blue Sky'
    - *Graptoveria* 'Debbie'
    - *Echeveria* 'Lilacina'
    - *Echeveria* 'Perle Von Nürnberg' ('PVN')
- 25 (2" [5-cm]) pots *Graptosedum* 'California Sunset' (with at least 2 heads per pot)
- 2 (2" [5-cm]) pots *Sedum* 'Donkey Tail' (with at least 2 heads per pot)

Craft and Arrange

1. Start by separating all the *Graptosedum* 'California Sunset' heads and remove the soil from all the mini succulents, leaving just the stems. Cut the reindeer sheet moss into 3-inch (7.5-cm) square pieces and the ribbon moss into 3-inch (7.5-cm) strips, making 11 of each. Add hot glue to the back of a square or strip of moss, then place the moss onto a cupcake holder, alternating between the reindeer moss and ribbon moss. For the top of the cupcake stand, I used half a square of the ribbon moss and half a square of the reindeer sheet moss.

3

2. To attach the succulents to the cupcake stand, add hot glue on top of the moss, then add the succulent stem on top of the glue, and then add additional glue on top of the stem. Quickly cover the stem with reindeer moss. I used the same color reindeer moss as the color of the sheet or ribbon moss on the cupcake stand. Add all of the cupcakelike succulents to the cupcake holders, positioning them so all of their fronts face outward.

3. Once all of the cupcake holders are filled, add 2 heads of *Graptosedum* 'California Sunset' in between each succulent. These make perfect fillers and add pops of contrast next to pink, purple and green-hued succulents. On the top of the cupcake stand, I positioned 1 *Echeveria* 'Lolita' and 4 heads of *Sedum* 'Donkey Tail' mixed with 4 heads of *Graptosedum* 'California Sunset'. Each cupcake holder should contain one main plant (these are the cupcakelike succulents) and two filler plants ('California Sunset').

Care

Mist twice a week. As the succulents start to outgrow the stand, simply snip the overgrown succulents and reattach them back to the stand or plant them in soil.

SUCCULENT FRUIT BASKET

Fruit baskets always have unique characteristics and designs, which makes it exciting to find a reason to repurpose one into an arrangement. Succulent-filled fruit baskets are ideal for the kitchen table, kitchen island or as a house-warming gift! Whatever you choose to do with your arrangement, be sure to use *Senecio* 'String of Bananas' succulents, so your arrangement will be fruitful.

Supplies

- 1 medium coco liner (brown basket liner or palm mat)
- 1 (2-tiered) fruit basket
- Cactus soil

Plants

- 3 (4" [10-cm]) pots *Senecio* 'String of Bananas'
- 2 (4" [10-cm]) pots *Echeveria* 'Rosea'
- 2 (4" [10-cm]) pots *Echeveria* 'Cassyz Winter'
- 2 (4" [10-cm]) pots *Echeveria* 'Misty Lilac'
- 2 (4" [10-cm]) pots *Echeveria* 'Dusty Rose'
- 3 (4" [10-cm]) pots *Echeveria* 'Perle Von Nürnberg' ('PVN')
- 3 (4" [10-cm]) pots *Echeveria imbricata* 'Blue Rose'
- 2 (4" [10-cm]) pots *Echeveria* 'Lolita'
- 8 (2" [5-cm]) pots *Echeveria* 'Royalty Hercules'

Craft and Arrange

1. Line the inside of the fruit basket with small pieces of coco liner. Coco liner is easy to pull apart, so simply pulling variously sized pieces to line the basket is the easiest method. Next, fill the basket halfway with soil.

2. On the top level of the fruit basket, plant *Senecio* 'String of Bananas' (about 2 inches [5 cm] thick) all around the edge, so they are cascading down the entire basket. Next, plant 1 *Echeveria* 'Rosea', 1 *Echeveria* 'Cassyz Winter', 1 *Echeveria* 'Misty Lilac' and 1 *Echeveria* 'Dusty Rose' in the top basket, placing them next to one another. In the bottom basket, plant 2 *Echeveria* 'PVN' and the remaining 'Rosea' in the center of the basket. Arrange the *Echeveria imbricata* 'Blue Rose', 'Cassyz Winter', 'Lolita', 'Misty Lilac' and 'Dusty Rose' in the bottom basket, alternating light and dark colors. In each gap between the *Echeverias*, plant the small *Echeveria* 'Royalty Hercules' succulents, filling all the spaces with full plants.

Care

Gently mist the entire arrangement twice a week. Since the succulents are all planted on top of coco liner, I recommend watering somewhere the water can drip off of it. If these succulents are kept inside permanently, bring the arrangement outside for an afternoon of sun once per week. This will ensure that the vibrant colors of the succulents stay fresh.

SUCCULENT WINEGLASS

Wineglasses make the perfect layered living terrarium! In this arrangement, layer moss, gravel and succulents to create a wineglass terrarium! With endless layering options, wineglasses can be made in any style, showcasing a variety of looks. Toast your next wine party with these living wineglasses and send guests home with these as party favors. Or try hosting a succulent sip & DIY and entertain your guests by having them craft their own terrariums!

Supplies

- Large wineglass
- 2 oz (55 g) white sand (craft sand, not beach sand)
- 2 oz (55 g) gravel
- 2 oz (55 g) sphagnum moss
- 2 oz (55 g) light green preserved reindeer moss
- 2 oz (55 g) cactus soil
- Chopsticks or small garden spade, for arranging

Plants

- 1 (2" [5-cm] pot) *Pachyphytum oviferum* 'Pink Moonstones'
- 1 (2" [5-cm] pot) *Echeveria* 'Lola'
- 1 (2" [5-cm] pot) *Aeonium* 'Sunburst'

Craft and Arrange

1. At the bottom of the wineglass, place the white sand, followed by the gravel and then some of the sphagnum moss. Gently position half of the reindeer moss on top, leaving a 2-inch (5-cm) hole in the middle.

Stylish Succulent Designs & Other Botanical Crafts

2b

2. Add a small amount of soil in the hole between the sphagnum moss and reindeer moss. Into the soil, plant the trio of succulents using the chopsticks or small shovel to ensure they are secure. On top of the soil, add small pieces of the remaining reindeer moss.

Care

Lightly mist the succulents twice a week. Since there aren't any drainage holes in the glass, it is crucial to not overwater the succulents. The sand and gravel layers act as natural drainage for water filtration. It is crucial not to use sand that is from the beach in this arrangement as the salt from the ocean will slowly deteriorate the succulents.

Note: Try filling a charming coffee mug with succulents, like a cactus coffee mug! In the arrangement shown below, I used *Graptoveria* 'Opalina', *Peperomia* 'Ruby Cascade', *Sedeveria* 'Lilac Mist' and *Crassula argentea variegata* 'White Jade'.

2c

SUCCULENT BAMBOO SALAD BOWL

Bamboo bowls are a great accent piece for any style of decor. With their smooth finish and natural wood marks, bamboo bowls make a great home for succulents! In this project, design a "salad" of succulents with dark purple succulents representing red romaine, green succulents as lettuce wedges and *Senecio* 'String of Pearls' acting as peas.

Supplies

- Medium bamboo salad bowl
- Water sealant spray
- Cactus soil

Plants

- 2 (6" [15-cm]) pots *Aeonium* 'Salad Bowl Green'
- 4 (4" [10-cm]) pots *Anacampseros rufescens*
- 2 (6" [15-cm]) pots *Senecio* 'String of Pearls'

Craft and Arrange

1. Spray the bamboo bowl with water sealant and let it dry. Fill the bowl two-thirds of the way with soil.

2. Starting in the center of the bowl, position 2 *Aeonium* 'Salad Bowl Green' succulents side by side. To the right and left side of each 'Salad Bowl Green', plant a pot of *Anacampseros rufescens* (4 pots in total), fluffing them as you plant them. In between each set of *Anacampseros rufescens*, plant a pot of *Senecio* 'String of Pearls', cascading over the sides of the bowl.

Care

Mist the succulents twice a week. The succulents used here thrive in indirect or bright light, but not direct sun.

TILLANDSIA PICTURE FRAME

Whether you are transforming an old and outdated picture frame or using a new one, this craft is excellent for all! This project incorporates a selection of natural mosses and rocks, combined with a living *Tillandsia* pictured in the center. These frames display beautifully between a collection of photographs, as coffee table accents or as an exquisite handmade gift.

Supplies

- 1 (5" x 7" [12.5 x 18-cm]) picture frame
- Hot glue gun and glue sticks
- 2 oz (55 g) natural bark moss
- 2 oz (55 g) polished river rocks (I used blue hues)
- 2 oz (55 g) light tan preserved Spanish moss
- 2 oz (55 g) dark green preserved forest moss
- 2 oz (55 g) light green preserved reindeer moss
- Small piece of driftwood (3" to 4" [7.5 to 10 cm])
- Fine scissors

Plants

- 1 small *Tillandsia xerographica* (2" to 3" [5 to 7.5 cm])

Craft and Arrange

1. Starting in the bottom right corner of the frame, add hot glue, then quickly cover with the bark moss, creating a diagonal section. Starting in the bottom left corner, plan out a small pathway of 6 to 8 river rocks in a diagonal direction toward the bark moss, interchanging the rocks to accommodate larger or smaller sizes, connecting them like a puzzle. Glue the rocks to the frame.

3b

2. Above the rocks on the left side of the frame, attach the Spanish moss to the frame with glue, filling about two-thirds of the height of the frame. Above the Spanish moss, adhere the forest moss, filling to the top of the frame, completing the left-hand side. To the right of the forest moss, add the reindeer moss, gluing it down, filling in the rest of the frame. Locate the center of the frame, then glue the driftwood in an upward diagonal direction (from right to left) onto the moss.

3. Add glue above the driftwood, then place the *Tillandsia xerographica* directly onto the glue, securing it to the frame. To finish the arrangement, use a fine pair of scissors to snip the edges of the moss, creating a clean and crisp border for the frame.

Care

All of the mosses used in this arrangement are preserved, so no care is needed for them. To care for the *Tillandsia xerographica*, simply mist the air plant twice a week. *Xerographica* do not need a lot of light, so they are the ideal air plant to keep inside, though they also thrive in bright light locations. *Xerographica* are slow growers, so it will take a couple of years to outgrow the frame!

Note: Also try creating this arrangement using a moss frame (shown on the left) to add another texture! On this moss frame, I used *Tillandsia tenuifolia* 'Emerald Forest'.

Traditional Gardens & OTHER PLANT FRIENDS

In this chapter, traditional garden planters are transformed into works of art. Learn to make unique Succulent Hexagons (page 149), or layer tall cylindrical vases planted with sansevierias (page 143). Here we go beyond just succulents and feature a few plant friends, such as orchids, tropical plants, sansevierias and lithops. Discover the unique "living stones" planted in the Lithop Living Stone Heart (page 139). Also featured in this chapter is one of my favorite plant projects, Tropical Foliage Kokedama (page 151).

SUCCULENT ORCHID TRIO ARRANGEMENT

This planted arrangement is perfect for fresh floral lovers, but it can also be enjoyed long after the orchids are finished blooming. Fill a large basin with a trio of orchids and pink, purple and blue succulents, creating a lush, living planter.

Supplies

- Large metal basin, to plant in
- Cactus soil
- Mini garden shovel

Plants

- 1 small *Phalaenopsis* 'Light Pink', left in its plastic sleeve with orchid bark
- 1 small *Phalaenopsis* 'Purple', left in its plastic sleeve with orchid bark
- 1 small *Phalaenopsis* 'Spotted Purple', left in its plastic sleeve with orchid bark
- 1 (4" [10-cm]) pot *Graptopetalum paraguayense* 'Hybrid'
- 1 (6" [15-cm]) pot *Echeveria* 'Afterglow'
- 1 (4" [10-cm]) pot *Echeveria* 'Etna'
- 2 (4" [10-cm]) pots *Pachyveria* 'Powder Puff' (with at least 2 heads)
- 2 (6" [15-cm]) pots *Echeveria* 'Lola'
- 2 (6" [15-cm]) pots *Echeveria* 'Violet Queen' (clusters with several heads)
- 2 (4" [10-cm]) pots *Sedum clavatum*

Craft and Arrange

1. Fill the basin one-third of the way with soil. Next, make three small holes in the soil for the orchids, then place them with their plastic sleeve. Arrange the trio with the lightest orchid in the center, surrounded by the purple orchids. Then, add soil all around the orchids' plastic sleeves, filling the basin three-quarters full.

1a

1b

2

2. Plant the *Graptopetalum paraguayense* 'Hybrid' in the center of the basin, under the lightest orchid. Plant the *Echeveria* 'Afterglow' under the 'Hybrid' on one side of the basin, and plant the *Echeveria* 'Etna' on the other side of the basin in the center.

3. Moving to the left from the 'Afterglow', plant 1 pot of *Pachyveria* 'Powder Puff' and 1 *Echeveria* 'Lola', followed by 1 *Echeveria* 'Violet Queen', wrapping around the edge. Plant 1 pot of *Sedum clavatum* on each side of the 'Etna', then the remaining 'Violet Queen' on the other side moving toward the left, wrapping around the other edge. Complete the arrangement with the remaining 'Lola' and remaining pot of 'Powder Puff'.

Care

To care for the succulents and orchid, mist twice a week. A general rule of thumb for most orchids is 2 ounces (60 ml) of water every week. For this arrangement, misting will suffice for the combination of the plants. Keep this arrangement in a bright-light location, out of direct sunlight. My favorite place to keep orchids is by a kitchen window. Once the orchid is done flowering (they usually flower for 2 months), snip the stem where the flowers were blooming, at the very bottom near the leaves. Orchids typically bloom 1 or 2 times per year, so with proper care, the orchid will flower again. If you prefer to have just the succulents, simply remove the orchid from the pot, fill any extra room with soil and spread the succulents evenly around.

LITHOP LIVING STONE HEART

Lithops, also known as "living stones," are extremely slow growing succulents with a rocklike look. Native to South Africa, *Lithops* were given their name from the Greek word *lithos*, meaning "stone," and *ops*, meaning "face," or Stone Face. In this project, learn how to arrange living stones. For this craft, I chose pots of *Lithops* with clusters of multiheads. The plant count will differ working with single heads, so please plan accordingly.

Supplies

- Heart-shaped terra-cotta pot
- Cactus soil
- Chopstick or tweezers
- Natural pumice
- Bristle brush

Plants

- 2 (2" [5-cm]) pots *Pleiospilos nelii* 'Royal Flush'
- 4 (2" [5-cm]) pots *Lithops spp.* 'Green'
- 4 (2" [5-cm]) pots *Lithops spp.* 'Brown Stone Faces'
- 3 (2" [5-cm]) pots *Lapidaria margaretae*
- 4 (2" [5-cm]) pots *Lithops spp.* 'Gray'
- 2 (2" [5-cm]) pots *Argyroderma*

Craft and Arrange

1. Fill the heart-shaped pot halfway with soil. Next, split all multiheads of the plants being used.

2. Starting in the bottom center of the heart, plant 1 *Pleiospilos nelii* 'Royal Flush'. Also, plant 1 'Royal Flush' in the top center of the heart. At the bottom of the heart, to the left of the 'Royal Flush' and working upward, plant 3 *Lithops spp.* 'Green', then 2 *Lithops spp.* 'Brown Stone Faces'. Next, plant 1 *Lapidaria margaretae*, 1 'Green' and 3 *Lithops spp.* 'Gray'. Add 1 larger-headed 'Brown Stone Faces', along with a cluster of 3 'Gray' and 1 *Argyroderma*. Fill in the remaining space to meet the edges of the 'Royal Flush' with 'Gray', 'Brown Stone Faces' and 'Green.'

2a

2b

3. In any open spaces, add any mini heads of the *Lithops* that are left over. Finally, using the chopsticks or the tweezers, sprinkle pumice over all spaces that show soil. Clean up the arrangement with the brush by lightly sweeping any excess residue away.

Care

Lithops do not like a lot of water. Since *Lithops* have dormant seasons, it is best to research your growing zone to discover how to best care for your *Lithops*.

Note: Also try planting *Lithops* in a small planter, such as the mini heart-shaped terra-cotta pot below!

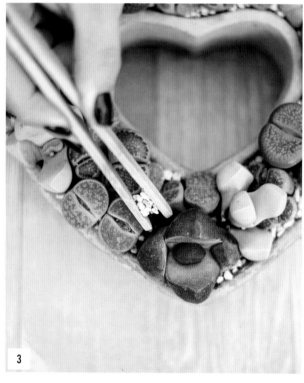

3

SANSEVIERIA LAYERED VASE

Layered with a variety of stones, moss and bark, sansevieria vases make the perfect decor! These cylindrical vases are topped with an arrangement of living sansevieria plants and finished with *Senecio* 'String of Pearls' circling the peak. Sansevierias are commonly referred to as "snake plants" or "mother in-law's tongue." Pairing sansevierias with succulents makes easy-to-care-for, visually appealing arrangements.

Supplies

- Cylindrical clear glass vase (9" [23 cm] tall and 3" [8 cm] in diameter)
- 3 oz (85 g) medium light-colored river rocks
- 3 oz (85 g) forest green preserved reindeer moss
- 3 oz (85 g) small light-colored river rocks
- 3 oz (85 g) spring light green preserved reindeer moss
- 3 oz (85 g) natural bark moss
- 3 oz (85 g) green preserved Spanish moss
- 3 oz (85 g) cactus soil
- Chopstick, for arranging
- 3 oz (85 g) tan preserved Spanish moss

Plants

- 1 (4" [10-cm]) pot *Sansevieria laurentii*
- 1 (4" [10-cm]) pot *Sansevieria* 'Black Coral'
- 1 (6" [15-cm]) pot *Senecio* 'String of Pearls'

Craft and Arrange

1. Place the medium-sized river rocks in the bottom of the glass vase, followed by the forest green reindeer moss. On top of those layers, add the small river rocks, then the light green reindeer moss. Next, add the bark moss and green Spanish moss, filling the entire vase.

1

2

2. Using your fingers, gently press the center of the green Spanish moss, pulling it to the sides of the vase, creating a pocket to plant in. Remove all the soil from the roots of each plant. Plant the *Sansevieria laurentii* and the *Sansevieria* 'Black Coral' in the small opening of the moss. Cover their roots with soil, adding enough to reach the top of the vase. The chopstick can be used to help keep the plants in place.

3. Next, add the tan Spanish moss all around the bottom of the plants, using the chopstick to nudge the moss into the arrangement. Finish by adding the *Senecio* 'String of Pearls', covering the circumference of the vase. Use the chopstick to thrust the 'String of Pearls' cuttings into the soil, and add extra tan Spanish moss to secure the pearls, if necessary.

Care

Mist very gently once a week. Since the plants live in a shallow area, very little water is needed. If during the warmer months the arrangement seems dry, mist twice a week. Sansevierias thrive in low-light areas, as their leaves can get sunburned with direct sun. A kitchen window is ideal for the light requirements for both plants.

3

SUCCULENT POTTED ORCHID ARRANGEMENT

The charming partnership of succulents and orchids is displayed in this arrangement. The delicate white orchid cascades overtop the pink and purple succulents planted at its base. An elegant pot elevates the arrangement to give additional height, creating a beautiful eye-catching piece.

Supplies

- 1 (8" [20.5-cm]) pot
- Cactus soil
- Mini shovel
- Chopstick, for arranging

Plants

- 1 large *Phalaenopsis* 'White', in its plastic sleeve with orchid bark
- 1 (6" [15-cm]) pot *Echeveria* 'Perle Von Nürnberg' ('PVN')
- 1 (6" [15-cm]) pot *Echeveria* 'Neon Breaker'
- 2 (4" [10-cm]) pot *Pachyveria* 'Powder Puff' (with at least 2 heads)
- 2 (2" [5-cm]) pots *Echeveria* 'Lilacina'
- 1 (4" [10-cm]) pot *Echeveria* 'Elegans'

Craft and Arrange

1. Fill the pot halfway with soil. Next, place the *Phalaenopsis* 'White' (with its plastic sleeve) on top of the soil in the center. Using a mini shovel, add additional soil around the edges of the orchid, filling the pot up three-quarters of the way.

2

2. Starting with the 2 large succulents, remove excess soil from their roots, then plant the *Echeveria* 'PVN' on 1 side of the orchid and the *Echeveria* 'Neon Breaker' on the other side. To plant the succulents, dig a small hole with the chopstick, and place the roots inside the hole. Use the chopstick to secure the roots and to help plant additional succulents in close proximity to each other.

3. Add 1 *Pachyveria* 'Powder Puff' to either side of the 'PVN' and 1 *Echeveria* 'Lilacina' to either side of the 'Neon Breaker'. In the empty space between the leaves of the 'PVN', plant the *Echeveria* 'Elegans' to fill in any holes.

Care

Mist the succulents and orchid twice a week. A general rule of thumb for most orchids is 2 ounces (60 ml) of water every week. For this arrangement, misting will suffice for the combination of the plants. Keep this arrangement in a bright-light location, out of direct sunlight. My favorite place to keep orchids is by a kitchen window. Once the orchid is done flowering (they usually flower for 2 months), snip the stem where the flowers were blooming at the very bottom near the leaves. Orchids typically bloom 1 or 2 times per year, so with proper care, the orchid will flower again. If you prefer to have just the succulents, simply remove the orchid from the pot, fill any extra room with soil and spread the succulents evenly around.

Note: Try making the same arrangement with fresh-cut orchids instead of a planted orchid for an alternative look (shown on the left). Add cut orchid stems in water in floral stem water picks (also known as water tubes, floral tubes, floral picks and flower spikes). Add these picks in between the succulents. Once a week, replace the water and snip the bottom off the stem to refresh. Orchid blooms will last about 3 to 4 weeks like this and then can be removed to enjoy the succulent arrangement or replenished. *Phalaenopsis* 'Sesame' were used in the pictured succulent arrangement.

SUCCULENT HEXAGONS

Hexagons have become trendy for home decor, and planting succulents inside a hexagon is elevating it to the next level! These classic hexagons pair wonderfully with colorful cascading succulents.

Supplies

- 1 (14" x 14" [35.5 x 35.5-cm]) wooden hexagon, or wood boards and plywood to create one
- Wood stain (I used brown) and paintbrush
- Cactus soil
- Mini shovel

Plants

- 2 (4" [10-cm]) pots *Sedum* 'Donkey Tail'
- 1 (4" [10-cm]) pot *Echeveria* 'Perle Von Nürnberg' ('PVN')
- 1 (4" [10-cm]) pot *Graptosedum* 'Blue Giant Hybrid' (with at least 2 heads)
- 2 (2" [5-cm]) pots *Echeveria* 'Neon Breaker'
- 2 (2" [5-cm]) pots *Echeveria* 'Dusty Rose'
- 1 (1-gal [4-L]) pot *Xerosicyos danguyi* 'String of Coins'
- 2 (2" [5-cm]) pots *Echeveria* 'Petra's Perle'

Craft and Arrange

1. Stain the hexagon with the wood stain. (I used a premade wooden hexagon for this craft, but to create your own, simply nail together various pieces of wood board or plywood in the shape of a hexagon—each piece is about 14 inches [35.5 cm]. Next, attach an additional piece of plywood to cover the bottom half of each side of the hexagon, making the planter area. Another alternative is to reach out to a local woodsmith with a photo of what you want.) After the hexagon is dry, fill three-quarters of the bottom with soil.

2. Starting in the center of the hexagon, place 1 pot of *Sedum* 'Donkey Tail' on either side of the hexagon. (They are easier to plant when you break apart the various heads in the pot.) Next, add the *Echeveria* 'PVN' in the middle of the 2 pots of 'Donkey Tail'.

3. On either side of the 'PVN', add 1 *Graptosedum* 'Blue Giant Hybrid', followed by 1 *Echeveria* 'Neon Breaker'. After these, add 1 'Dusty Rose' on each side. Next, plant 1 head of *Xerosicyos danguyi* 'String of Coins' in all 4 corners of the hexagon's planting area. Finish the arrangement by planting the remaining *Echeveria* 'Petra's Perle' in the last space of the hexagon on each side.

Care

Gently mist with water twice a week. Since there is no drainage hole in the bottom of the hexagon, it is crucial not to overwater, as it can cause the succulents to flood and drown. It is best to keep this arrangement in an area with bright but indirect light.

TROPICAL FOLIAGE KOKEDAMA

Kokedamas are an ancient Japanese form of living moss art, commonly in the shape of a sphere. Most types of plants can live in kokedamas. This project uses three house plants. In typical floral arranging and plantscaping, it is best to use a thriller, a filler and a spiller plant. The thriller plant is the most vibrant and eye-catching—in this case, the *Anthurium* 'Pink'—whereas the filler plant is usually larger and leafier, taking up more room in the arrangement. The *Maranta leuconeura* 'Red Prayer Plant' acts as the filler here. The spiller plant spills over the side of the arrangement, as the *Calathea roseupicta* does here. Since an odd number of plants is always best in floral arranging, I suggest using all three with varying types of leaves in the kokedama arrangement. It is crucial to pair together plants that have similar needs for light and moisture.

Supplies

- 1 (8½" x 20" [21.5 x 50-cm]) sheet white tulle or mesh
- 2 packages sheet moss, or 1 large package, cut into two 14" x 8" (35.5 x 20.5-cm) pieces
- Misting bottle filled with water
- 1 spool of clear fishing line

Plants

- 1 (4" [10-cm]) pot *Anthurium* 'Pink'
- 1 (4" [10-cm]) pot *Maranta leuconeura* 'Red Prayer Plant'
- 1 (4" [10-cm]) pot *Calathea roseupicta*

Craft and Arrange

1. Place the sheet of tulle flat on a working surface. Place the first sheet of moss flat on top of the tulle. Carefully remove the plants from their growing pots, then place the plants on top of the tulle. The soil and roots of the plants should be centered as a trio in the middle of the tulle. Gently mist all around the soil with water, then mold the 3 plants together by gently pressing on the sides of the soil.

1a

1b

1c

2

3a

3b

4a

4b

4c

2. Lift up the far right and far left sides of the tulle (with the moss on top of it), bringing it to the base of the plants. It should be tulle on the outside, then moss, then the plants. Make sure that the tulle is just underneath the bottom leaves of the 3 plants. The tulle will just cover the soil, not the plants themselves. If there is excess tulle, have it stick straight up for the next step.

3. Wrap the fishing line underneath the bottom leaves of the arrangement, around the entire trio of plants. Now, tie a double knot with the loose end of the fishing line. (It is easiest to keep the fishing line connected to the spool, so you will not cut it too short.) With the fishing line still attached to the spool, start wrapping it around the tulle cluster. The purpose of wrapping the cluster with fishing line is to hold the plants inside the moss-lined tulle. Wrap the fishing line about 30 times around the tulle cluster in all directions, creating a spherical shape. Do not cut the fishing line when done with this step; keep it attached to the spool. Cut away any excess tulle that is above the lowest leaves of the plants. Just the roots and soil of the plants need to be covered.

4. Once the tulle is securely wrapped with fishing line, place the next sheet moss layer down flat. If the moss you are using has one green side and one nongreen side, place the green side down toward your working surface. Gently mist the sheet moss with water. Place the tulle cluster on top of the next layer of moss. Slowly, start to lift the sheet of moss up, toward the tulle cluster. Gently mold the sheet moss, covering the entire tulle cluster with moss. Mold the cluster into a spherical shape with a flat bottom. Once the sheet moss is all around the tulle, completely covering the cluster, starting with the loose end of the fishing line, wrap the attached fishing line around the outside of the moss, using the same method as before. Wrap about 20 times. When finished, cut the fishing line with about 5 inches (12.5 cm) extra. Take the loose end of the fishing line and double-knot it to one of the fishing lines wrapped around the moss. Cut the end short so it does not show.

Care

Place the bottom of the kokedama in a small bucket of water two times a week for 10 minutes. Most tropical foliage and indoor plants need to be kept out of direct sunlight, so choose a place in your home where there is low, indirect light. I recommend keeping this arrangement on either a plate or something with a lining so that the wet moss does not stick to surfaces.

Note: An alternative craft method can be done with a succulent or a single plant (as shown below). Simply follow the same crafting instructions and wrap the moss around your favorite plant. If you choose to use succulents, echeverias work the best!

Pictured is a 6-inch (15-cm) *Echeveria* 'Ruffles'.

DESERT-INSPIRED PLANTER

This planter is inspired by the desert, but without all the pricks and thorns! All the plants in this project resemble the natural look of cacti. This is a perfect way to re-create those desert vibes without the painful cacti.

Supplies

- Cement planter
- Cactus soil
- Chopsticks and small garden spade, for arranging

Plants

- 1 (4" [10-cm]) pot *Aloe striata* 'Coral Aloe'
- 2 (4" [10-cm]) pots *Euphorbia flanaganii* 'Medusa's Head'
- 2 (2" [5-cm]) pots *Anacampseros rufescens*
- 1 (4" [10-cm]) pot *Faucaria tigrina* 'Tiger Jaws'
- 1 (4" [10-cm]) pot *Cremnosedum* 'Little Gem'
- 1 (2" [5-cm]) pot *Echeveria purpusorum*
- 1 (4" [10-cm]) pot *Senecio haworthii* 'Cocoon Plant' (with multiple heads)
- 1 (2" [5-cm]) pot *Titanopsis calcarea*
- 1 (4" [10-cm]) pot *Orostachys japonica* 'Rock Pine'
- 2 (2" [5-cm]) pots *Fenestraria* 'Baby Toes'
- 1 (4" [10-cm]) pot *Gasteria* 'Little Warty'

Craft and Arrange

1. Fill the cement planter halfway with soil.

2. Starting in the center of the planter, plant the *Aloe striata* 'Coral Aloe' and then 1 *Euphorbia flanaganii* 'Medusa's Head' on each side of it. In front of the 'Coral Aloe', add 1 *Anacampseros rufescens*, then in front of that, plant the *Faucaria tigrina* 'Tiger Jaws'. Separate the *Cremnosedum* 'Little Gem' into 3 equal clusters. Plant 1 on the right side of the 'Tiger Jaws' and 1 on the left side. On the right side of 'Little Gem', add the *Echeveria purpusorum*. Separate the *Senecio haworthii* 'Cocoon Plant' into 2 equal clusters, and add 1 cluster in each space between the 'Coral Aloe' and the 'Medusa's Head'. This should fill the first half of the planter.

2a

2b

3. In the next half, working around the 'Coral Aloe', plant the remaining *Anacampseros rufescens*, followed by the *Titanopsis calcarea* and the *Orostachys japonica* 'Rock Pine'. Working outward, starting underneath the *Anacampseros rufescens*, plant 1 pot of *Fenestraria* 'Baby Toes', then the *Gasteria* 'Little Warty' and then the remaining 'Baby Toes'. Fill in any gaps with the remaining *Cremnosedum* 'Little Gem'.

Care

This planter was designed to be kept on an outdoor patio table, with covered, indirect light. Mist it with water once a week if the planter does not have any drain holes, or twice a week if it does have drain holes.

Note: Try planting other desert-inspired succulents in a cactus-shaped planter! Pictured below are *Graptopetalum bellum* and *Anacampseros telephiastrum variegata* 'Sunrise'.

Visual Plant List

Succulents

Thousands of unique succulents are grown throughout the world, ranging in color, size, shape and variation. I did my best to accurately label the succulent names, but some regions may refer to various succulents by different names. Please refer to their botanical name for correct identification. I recommend Debra Lee Baldwin's succulent books as a reference, as she outlines species of succulents in-depth. Jeff Moore has also authored a number of succulent books that are great references for identification and growing tips. Here is a visual list of all the succulents used in *Stylish Succulent Designs & Other Botanical Crafts*.

	Aeonium 'Emerald Ice'
	Aeonium 'Kiwi'
	Aeonium 'Mardi Gras'
	Aeonium 'Salad Bowl Green'
	Aeonium 'Sunburst'
	Aeonium 'Fiesta'

	Aloe striata 'Coral Aloe'
	Anacampseros rufescens
	Anacampseros telephiastrum variegata 'Sunrise'
	Argyroderma
	Ceropegia woodii 'String of Hearts'
	Corpuscularia lehmannii 'Ice Plant'
	Cotyledon 'Chalk Fingers'

	Cotyledon pendens 'Cliff Cotyledon'
	Cotyledon variegata 'Bear Paws Variegated'
	Crassula 'String of Buttons'
	Crassula 'Tom Thumb'
	Crassula argentea variegata 'White Jade'
	Crassula ovata 'Dwarf Jade Plant'
	Crassula perforata variegata
	Crassula platyphylla
	Crassula platyphylla variegata
	Crassula pubescebs radicans 'Cranberry Crumbles'

	Crassula rubricaulis 'Candy Cane'
	Crassula rupestris
	Cremnosedum 'Little Gem'
	Echeveria harmsii 'Ruby Slippers'
	Echeveria 'Afterglow'
	Echeveria 'Andromeda'
	Echeveria 'Blue Atoll'
	Echeveria 'Blue Bird'
	Echeveria 'Blue Curls'
	Echeveria 'Blue Hybrid'

	Echeveria 'Blue Prince'
	Echeveria 'Blue Sky Ruffle Hybrid'
	Echeveria 'Blue Sky'
	Echeveria 'Blue'
	Echeveria 'Cassyz Winter'
	Echeveria 'Cubic Frost'
	Echeveria 'Dusty Rose'
	Echeveria 'Elegans'
	Echeveria 'Etna'
	Echeveria 'Hawaii'

	Echeveria 'Lilacina'
	Echeveria 'Lolita'
	Echeveria 'Minima'
	Echeveria 'Misty Lilac'
	Echeveria 'Neon Breaker'
	Echeveria 'Parva'
	Echeveria 'Perle von Nürnberg' ('PVN')
	Echeveria 'Petra's Perle'
	Echeveria 'Princess Lace'
	Echeveria 'Prolifica'

Echeveria 'Pulidonis'	Echeveria 'Topsy Turvy'
Echeveria 'Pulv-Oliver'	Echeveria 'Violet Queen'
Echeveria 'Purple Pearl'	Echeveria 'White'
Echeveria 'Raindrops'	Echeveria 'Galaxy Blue'
Echeveria 'Rosea'	Echeveria 'Lime N Chile'
Echeveria 'Royalty Hercules'	Echeveria 'Painted Lady'
Echeveria 'Ruffles'	Echeveria 'Pink Ruffle Hybrid'
Echeveria 'Sahara'	Echeveria imbricata 'Blue Rose'
Echeveria 'Sanyatwe'	Echeveria 'Lola'
Echeveria 'Subsessilis'	Echeveria purpusorum

Echeveria setosa 'Mexican Firecracker'	Graptosedum 'Blue Giant Hybrid'
Echeveria setosa variegata deminuta 'Firecracker Plant'	Graptosedum 'California Sunset'
Euphorbia flanaganii 'Medusa's Head'	Graptoveria 'Blue Pearl'
Faucaria tigrina 'Tiger Jaws'	Graptoveria 'Debbie'
Fenestraria 'Baby Toes'	Graptoveria 'Fred Ives'
Gasteria 'Little Warty'	Graptoveria 'Jules'
Graptopetalum bellum	Graptoveria 'Opalina'
Graptopetalum paraguayense 'Ghost Plant'	Graptoveria 'Platinum'
Graptopetalum paraguayense 'Hybrid'	Kalanchoe 'Snow White Panda'
Graptopetalum superbum	Kalanchoe fedtschenkoi variegata

	Kalanchoe luciae variegata 'Fantastic'
	Kalanchoe millotii
	Kalanchoe tomentosa 'Light Panda Plant'
	Kalanchoe tomentosa 'Teddy Bear'
	Lapidaria margaretae
	Lithop spp. 'Brown Stone Faces'
	Lithops spp. 'Gray'
	Lithos spp. 'Green'
	Orostachys japonica 'Rock Pine'
	Oscularia deltoides
	Othonna capensis 'Ruby Necklace'
	Pachyphytum oviferum 'Pink Moonstones'
	Pachyveria 'Blue Mist'
	Pachyveria 'Powder Puff'
	Pachyveria 'Scheideckeri'
	Peperomia 'Ruby Cascade'
	Pleiospilos nelii 'Royal Flush'
	Portulacaria afra variegata 'Rainbow Bush'
	Sedeveria 'Blue Elf'
	Sedeveria 'Lilac Mist'

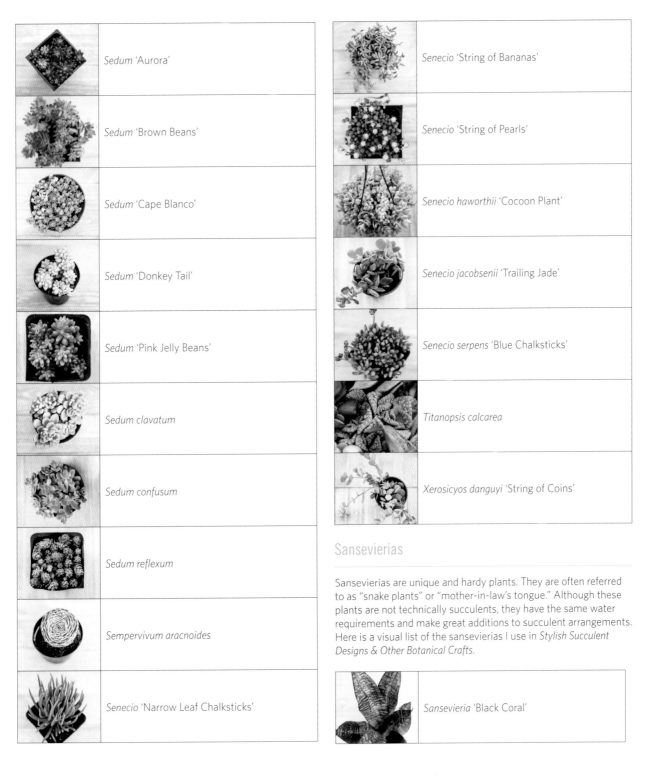

	Sedum 'Aurora'
	Sedum 'Brown Beans'
	Sedum 'Cape Blanco'
	Sedum 'Donkey Tail'
	Sedum 'Pink Jelly Beans'
	Sedum clavatum
	Sedum confusum
	Sedum reflexum
	Sempervivum aracnoides
	Senecio 'Narrow Leaf Chalksticks'

	Senecio 'String of Bananas'
	Senecio 'String of Pearls'
	Senecio haworthii 'Cocoon Plant'
	Senecio jacobsenii 'Trailing Jade'
	Senecio serpens 'Blue Chalksticks'
	Titanopsis calcarea
	Xerosicyos danguyi 'String of Coins'

Sansevierias

Sansevierias are unique and hardy plants. They are often referred to as "snake plants" or "mother-in-law's tongue." Although these plants are not technically succulents, they have the same water requirements and make great additions to succulent arrangements. Here is a visual list of the sansevierias I use in *Stylish Succulent Designs & Other Botanical Crafts*.

	Sansevieria 'Black Coral'

Sansevieria laurentii

Tillandsia (Air Plants)

Tillandsia plants, better known as "air plants," simply grow in the air—without any soil at all! They thrive in bright-light locations, but without harsh, direct sunlight. To care for these unique plants, simply mist the base of the plant with water twice a week. These are slow-growing plants and can be enjoyed for years to come. Here is a visual list of the air plants used in Stylish Succulent Designs & Other Botanical Crafts.

Tillandsia aeranthos 'Purple Fan'

Tillandsia brachycaulos

Tillandsia bulbosa

Tillandsia butzii

Tillandsia caput-medusae

Tillandsia harrisii

Tillandsia ionantha fuego

Tillandsia tenuifolia 'Emerald Forest'

Tillandsia velickiana

Tillandsia xerographica

Orchids

In this book I include two different orchid projects (pages 137 and 145). When the orchids are done blooming, trim the stem and let the succulents thrive around the orchid leaves. Here is a visual list of the orchids used in Stylish Succulent Designs & Other Botanical Crafts.

Phalaenopsis 'Light Pink'

Phalaenopsis 'Purple'

Phalaenopsis 'Sesame'

Phalaenopsis 'Spotted Purple'

Phalaenopsis 'White'

Tropical Plants

Tropical plants thrive on being kept moist, so these do not make good living partners for succulents. Here is a visual list of the plants used in *Stylish Succulent Designs & Other Botanical Crafts*.

	Anthurium 'Pink'
	Calathea roseopicta
	Maranta leuconeura 'Red Prayer Plant'

Mosses

Moss is a great complement to succulents for both decorative and planting purposes, and it comes in a variety of textures, colors and shapes. Here is a visual list of the mosses used in *Stylish Succulent Designs & Other Botanical Crafts*.

	Bark moss
	Forest moss (green)
	Mound moss (green)

	Reindeer moss (dark green)
	Reindeer moss (light green)
	Reindeer moss (medium green)
	Sheet moss (green)
	Sheet moss (natural color)
	Spanish moss (brown)
	Spanish moss (gray)
	Spanish moss (green)
	Spanish moss (tan)
	Sphagnum moss

Acknowledgments

I would like to graciously acknowledge my entire family for being by my side through the whole process of starting my business. Each one of my family members has contributed countless hours of help, encouragement and support to me.

Mom and Dad, thank you for raising me to be an entrepreneur and always encouraging the small businesses I started over the years. From making flower pens at age ten and selling loose-leaf tea in college, you were there through it all; you are my #1 fans! Thank you for also letting me operate my business out of your garage, and thank you for always cleaning up my messes and watering my plants when I get too busy.

Preston, my husband, thank you for always putting up with my spontaneous life and wild ideas, and for holding my hand every step of the way. Thank you for encouraging my creativity and helping me bring my imaginations to reality. Thank you for being right behind me to pick up every piece as it falls. You are honestly my life teammate, my other half and the perfect complement to me.

Grandma and Grandpa, thank you for letting me play in your garden from the beginning! I will always cherish the time we spent in the garden, which cultivated my curiosity with plants that I am now turning into my future! Thank you for always being a phone call away to bounce ideas off of and a quick drive down the freeway to see me at any given time!

I would like to thank **Flower Hill Promenade** in Del Mar (San Diego), California. Thank you, Leslie and Siena, for always saying yes to my installation ideas. Thank you for displaying my living art around the shopping plaza. Thank you for taking a chance on me. Thank you, Flower Hill, for hosting all of my photoshoots.

I would like to thank **Rachael Smith** of Rachael Smith Photography for photographing my entire book and making my vision come to life. Thank you for putting up with me during the blood, sweat and tears, late nights, craft store runs, grouchy early mornings and bizarre angles to get "the photo" and always making me feel so comfortable. Thank you for being my friend.

I would like to acknowledge **DM Color** in Vista, California, for allowing me to take photos at your succulent nurseries. Thank you to all of my 25-plus vendors for letting me ask you a million questions and take forever to choose my plants.

Thank you to all of my **followers**, **customers** and **fans**! I am so grateful that because of you, I am able to do what I love and inspire others to create! Thank you for supporting my small business and for teaching me when I didn't know! Thank you for your loyalty. I appreciate you all.

I acknowledge **Lilly Pulitzer**. Thank you for creating vibrant and colorful clothing that makes me feel so happy while playing in the garden. I proudly wore Lilly Pulitzer in each crafting photoshoot.

Thank you to my publisher, **Page Street Publishing**, for taking a chance on me, believing in me and giving me this opportunity.

Meet the Author

Jessica Cain grew up and currently lives in San Diego, California. Raised as an only child, Jessica lived a very hands-on childhood. From a young age, she took an interest in entrepreneurship, which is now channeled into her succulent business.

In 2016, after graduating from college, Jessica and her grandmother made their annual fall succulent pumpkins. After crafting, Jessica posted a photo of her pumpkin on social media and immediately generated a buzz. This is where her entire business began—completely by accident!

Playing with succulents had always been a hobby of hers, and it quickly became an obsession—anything that could be planted with succulents, she planted! After the buzz of fall 2016's succulent pumpkin extravaganza, in early 2017, she decided to launch online with only one product—succulent heart wreaths! Shortly after, she received an offer to sell her arrangements and crafts in a local San Diego storefront. It wasn't until October 2017 that she decided to acknowledge she had started a business and it was not a hobby any longer! In 2017, she learned to make a vast variety of arrangements and crafts, leading into her DIY parties.

During the bustling spring 2018 season with Easter and Mother's Day, she had been showcasing her living art arrangements at various craft shows and events, leading to her first TV appearance on Fox5 San Diego. Shortly after that, a local shopping center (Flower Hill Promenade, Del Mar) reached out, interested in having Jessica start a storefront. In June 2018, Jessica opened her first pop-up storefront, the Botanical Boutique, which was later featured on the CW San Diego. After closing the shop at the end of the year, she taught classes and designed custom arrangements, which were featured on KUSI San Diego.

Today, Jessica and her team showcase her arrangements throughout San Diego at various pop-up shopping bazaars. She teaches a variety of DIY plant party classes and manages her online e-commerce store, In Succulent Love, where she ships over 120 different succulents, DIY kits and arrangements. She has big plans to launch a monthly plant subscription box, the Plant Parcel, which will be a monthly box filled with various living plants.

Stay tuned to Jessica's botanical journey by following along on Instagram @InSucculentLove!

Index